ECHOES
From a Frozen Land

ECHOES
From a Frozen Land

DONALD B. MARSH

Edited by WINIFRED MARSH

Hurtig Publishers
Edmonton

Text copyright © 1987 by W.F. Marsh
Photographs copyright © 1974 by the estate of Donald Marsh

Hurtig Publishers Ltd.
10560—105 Street
Edmonton, Alberta
Canada T5H 2W7

Canadian Cataloguing in Publication Data

Marsh, Donald B. (Donald Ben), 1903–
    Echoes from a frozen land

ISBN 0-88830-322-X

    1. Marsh, Donald B. (Donald Ben), 1903–   2. Inuit — Northwest Territories — Eskimo Point — Missions — History.*   3. Church of England in Canada — Missions — Northwest Territories — Eskimo Point — History.
4. Missionaries — Northwest Territories — Biography.
5. Church of England in Canada — Clergy — Biography.
I. Marsh, Winifred Petchey.   II. Title.
BV2813.M37A3   1987   266′.3′0924   C87-091323-9

Maps: James Loates, illustrating

Printed and bound in Canada

CONTENTS

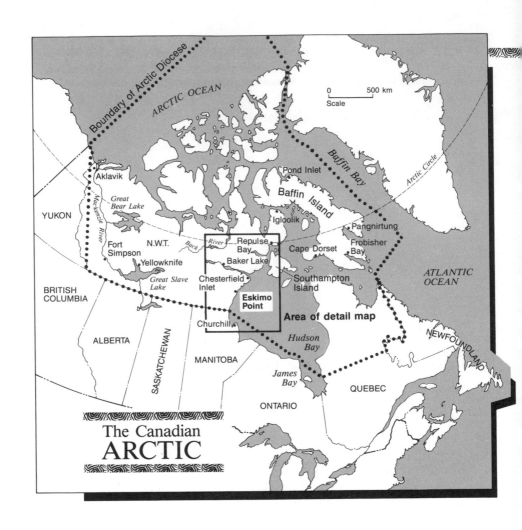

The Canadian
ARCTIC

The Area of
ESKIMO POINT

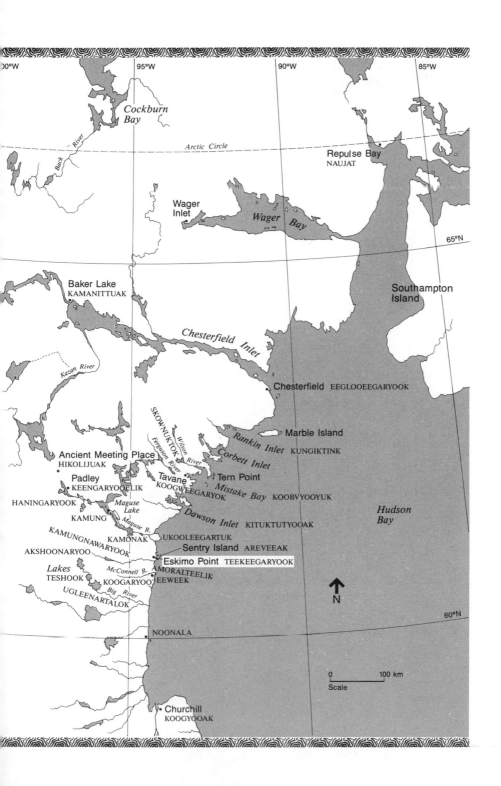

100°W   95°W   90°W   85°W

Cockburn Bay

Back River

Arctic Circle

Repulse Bay
NAUJAT

Wager Inlet

Wager Bay

65°N

Baker Lake
KAMANITTUAK

Southampton Island

Chesterfield Inlet

Kazan River

Chesterfield EEGLOOEEGARYOOK

SKOWNUKTOK

Rankin Inlet ○ Marble Island

Ferguson River Wilson River

Corbett Inlet KUNGIKTINK

Ancient Meeting Place
HIKOLIJUAK

Tern Point

Padley
KEENGARYOOELIK

Tavane
KOOGWEEGARYOK

Mistake Bay KOOBVYOOYUK

HANINGARYOOK

Maguse Lake

Dawson Inlet KITUKTUTYOOAK

Hudson Bay

KAMUNG

Maguse R.

KAMUNGNAWARYOOK   KAMONAK   UKOOLEEGARTUK

AKSHOONARYOO

Sentry Island AREVEEAK

Eskimo Point TEEKEEGARYOOK

Lakes
TESHOOK

McConnell R.

AMORALTEELIK

KOOGARYOO EEWEEK

UGLEENARTALOK

Big River

N

60°N

NOONALA

0   100 km
Scale

Churchill
KOOGYOOAK

Donald Marsh when he left for Eskimo Point in 1926 to establish a Christian mission. He stayed at Eskimo Point for eighteen years, subsequently becoming the second Anglican Bishop of the Diocese of the Arctic.

BY WINIFRED MARSH

INTRODUCTION

In the summer of 1926, Donald Ben Marsh, a twenty-three-year old novice missionary fresh from seminary in Saskatoon, set out alone with a few personal belongings for the north-western shore of Hudson Bay to establish a Christian mission at Eskimo Point. And for the next forty-seven years, until 1973, Donald Marsh lived closely with the Inuit. He became, in 1950, "Donald the Arctic," Anglican Bishop of the Diocese of the Arctic, following Archibald Lang Fleming, the first such bishop, who had begun his Arctic ministry in 1909. *Echoes from a Frozen Land* embraces the first eighteen years (1926 to 1943) of that forty-seven-year span, years in which Donald Marsh, as an Anglican missionary, lived with the Padlimiut Eskimos in the region surrounding Eskimo Point, Northwest Territories.

Donald traveled thousands of miles by dog team during winter hunting seasons to visit the widely scattered families in their igloos and provide health care, information on hygiene, news of the region, personal counseling, and, of course, to tell the story of the Christian gospel. In the early years of his ministry, Donald shared life in "the old way" with his Inuit friends in the igloos, and he soon learned to appreciate the wisdom of many of their traditions. But he saw the inexorably mounting pressures of southern institutions relentlessly working to alter the native northern way of life over the years, and he recognized his own role and respon-sibilities as an agent of cultural change.

The word *Eskimo* is a romantic and nostalgic term. It calls to mind images of vast, frozen plains, of the aurora borealis and polar bears, of igloos and parkas and sled dogs, of Roald Amundsen, Robert Peary, and Nanook of the North — and the Eskimo people themselves. Like most stereotypes, there is some measure of truth in the image, but also considerable overgeneralization, for each cultural group within any larger society may be as different from each other as cheese and ice cream. Moreover, and more importantly, times change. Northern life inevitably had to change. Indeed, the nomadic

11

life style has given way to established settlements; igloos have been replaced by prefabricated houses, dog teams by snowmobiles, kayaks by aluminum motorboats, and the list goes on.

Eskimo is an Algonquin word, with slightly derogatory undertones, meaning "eaters of raw meat." Today the term is obsolete. They call themselves — and prefer to be called — Inuit, simply meaning "the people" or "we people." (One male Eskimo is an "inuk," and one female is an "angnak." It is a misnomer to call a single male "an Inuit.") However, in the period 1926 to 1943, when Donald Marsh wrote down his musings and observations, massive material and cultural change had not yet taken place. Nor had it yet become fashionable to use the term "Inuit," and so that designation is seldom found in this compilation of his writings.

The Inuit who are the subject of this book claimed a huge territory north and west of Noonala along the western shores of Hudson Bay. They called themselves Padlimiut; some say the name derives from some hills in the approximate centre of their region, but others claim the name comes from willow bushes (*padlei*) that in this area grow in greater luxuriance than elsewhere.

Their life style before contact with white people is not too difficult to determine, because even a few years ago, up to about 1960, they lived almost entirely as they had done in the earliest days. Known to ethnologists as the Caribou Eskimos, the five tribes that comprised this group gained most of their livelihood from the Barren Lands caribou, which was indeed life to them. In contrast to almost all other Arctic tribes, they depended little on the sea for food. There were two exceptions — the coastal Padlimiut and the Shownukromiut, who lived just north of the Padlimiut along the shore of Hudson Bay. (Shownukromiut translates as "the bone people" and is said to be derived from a piece of land that was covered with bones.) Among the Padlimiut only these two tribes had some seaboard culture, and even so, they depended to a great degree on the caribou.

Explorers ventured into the far North, largely by sea, as early as the sixteenth century. As time went on, more and more hardy travelers, curious and courageous, penetrated Arctic waters in search of the Greenland whale, gold, and the Northwest Passage. But with the exception of a rare few, notably the Moravian missionaries from Europe, none stayed except to die locked in the ice in their ships.

The Moravians established missions in Labrador in 1771 but did not expand their activities into Arctic Canada. Other outposts of Christianity were founded during the nineteenth century around the shores of James and Hudson bays and were served by such intrepid missionaries as Bishop John Horden, Dr. Edmund J. Peck, Dr. W. G. "Reindeer" Walton, Bishop Joseph Lofthouse, Rev. Stewart of Ungava, Bishop Archibald Fleming, and others. However, as late as the 1920s there existed Inuit who lived within a radius of 250 miles from Eskimo Point, north of Fort Churchill, who had never heard the Christian gospel. And so it was that Donald Marsh set forth to establish in 1926 the first Anglican mission at Eskimo Point.

Donald's immigration from England to Canada — for enrolment at Emmanuel College in Saskatoon — came about through my family, the Petcheys of Winchmore Hill in London, England, who lived adjacent to his home in Enfield. The mothers of both families were friends involved in beekeeping and church activities. While on holiday in Devon in 1921, my mother and I happened to listen to a stirring sermon inviting all the young men in the congregation to go to Canada for training in missionary work. I was seventeen years old and a girl; thus, I was excluded from consideration, but the desire for foreign mission work lay deep within my heart. As I left the church that summer's night I was angry and resentful. Suddenly, I stood still and exclaimed, "Mother! Isn't that just what Don Marsh could do?" She wrote to him immediately, and even before we returned from our holidays Donald Marsh had sailed for Canada. Twelve years later I would join him at Eskimo Point as his bride. My mother wryly commented in later years, "Little did I know I was sending my own daughter."

Donald's mother became seriously ill in England in early 1926, at about the time that he was finishing his seminary study in Saskatoon. He was given a leave of absence on compassionate grounds to spend a few weeks at home, before he was to leave for the Arctic. My personal interest in him had never waned since he first set out for Canada three years earlier, and in the ensuing years we kept a close correspondence. In 1933, towards the end of a three-month furlough in England, we married and returned together to Eskimo Point. We could now share the great Arctic silence, sometimes together, sometimes apart when he made his lengthy winter and spring visitations.

During the times that Donald was gone for extended periods, I sensed a need to increase my daily activities. So I taught household crafts to some of the local Inuit, began learning and writing the Inuktitut language, painted the beautiful flowers and landscapes around Eskimo Point in watercolours and began to record in colour the Inuit beadwork designs; I also illustrated the Padlimiut medical book that Donald had written. Once a little boy peeked over my shoulder and saw my diagram of the human skeleton; in a bewildered voice he said, "Mrs. Marsh, what did you do with the meat?" Even early spring cleaning was good relaxation, and visits to igloo homes were occasions that forced me to go out, always bundled in my caribou furs. In 1937 we had a son, David, and then in 1940 a daughter, Rosemary, who was described by one Eskimo friend as "just like a little doll." But she failed to distinguish herself among the Eskimos, because she was a girl and therefore not a potential hunter. Valerie, our third child, was born in 1942.

The mechanics of daily living — such as melting ice or snow for water, cleaning and filling lamps for lighting, or making bread — occupied a lot of time and energy. These were the days before washing machines and dryers, gas or electric stoves, and the present-day multitude of children's toys. Without conventional toys our children grew up with creative abilities and a sensitivity towards nature, and later they developed as avid readers. We tried to be first and foremost a family, but it was sometimes difficult when Donald was away for extended periods. And as far as I was able, I tried always to be on hand to support my husband in the life work he had chosen and which had become mine also. To a certain extent, that work still absorbs me today.

Donald often sat by the light of an oil lamp in the house that he built himself and wrote of his experiences and observations among the people. He took copious notes, on whatever odd pieces of paper happened to be available, of information and stories that he intended later to flesh out. Frequently, however, there wasn't the opportunity to finish the notes, and when he died I was left with a prodigious quantity of his written material, some of which lacked dates

14

and important details necessary to its chronological understanding. I have been able, nevertheless, to fill in many of the gaps over these past few years.

Much of Donald's writings dealt with the face-to-face living experiences that he and the native Inuit together often enjoyed, often struggled through in the face of danger, and sometimes feared. Life was hard. For the first seven years at Eskimo Point he lived alone, and there were times that he wrote out of loneliness and introspection, when the world he had left behind seemed so very far away.

Realizing that he was witness to the onset of massive cultural change, he recorded what he could of the old ways; and because the Inuit considered him to be one of themselves, he experienced much of that life style. He wrote about changes brought about by traders and other white "intruders" into the far North, as well as about his own impact, as a missionary, on the Inuit. Some changes were good, others not so good. But always he had in mind the well-being of the people. He encouraged them, for example, to remain on the land as hunters and not be dependent upon trading posts for the goods of southern civilization. And he fought for them against government incursions upon their rights as citizens, knowing that they wished to remain Inuit.

Donald's ministry to the Inuit extended from 1926 until a short time before his untimely and accidental death in England in February, 1974, a total of forty-seven years. The words written in this book are basically his words, written at the time and in a mode of expression that reflects the time period (1926–43). The style is peculiarly his; some words and expressions are today considered Victorian and archaic, but they emanate largely from him and reflect his view from the mission house, in igloos, and on the trail. There is no definite historical sequence — nor even a specific chronology — in the text. Events that take place did so between 1926 and 1943; they are a slice of that time period. Donald recorded temperatures in the Fahrenheit scale and other measures, such as distance, in the imperial system; I've recorded these as he wrote them.

Since 1976 I have sorted through and edited the mass of information — both written and photographic — that he had collected during his life among the people of the North. The life style of those people has passed, but Donald's words and photos preserve an almost forgotten and special way of life.

At the time that Donald first penned these words at Eskimo Point, many of the comforts we enjoy today were not known, and some were not even invented. Donald's first radio was a home-made "cat's whisker" contraption around which one had to cup one's hands in order to attract signals and messages that were sent from radio stations in the South; it was commonly known as a crystal radio. In those days connection to the "outside world" was limited to the yearly supply ship (the *Nascopie*, out of Aberdeen, Scotland) which made calls at all Eastern Arctic outposts of the Hudson's Bay Company. The west coast of Hudson Bay was shallow, with many uncharted reefs, so that boats of smaller tonnage transferred supplies for Noonala, Eskimo Point, and points farther north from Churchill. A letter packet usually arrived by dog team in January. There were no mechanized vehicles, no roads, no electricity, no running water, no sewage disposal, no telephone or TV. The only buildings belonged to the white residents of a post: the Hudson's Bay Company, the missions, and later the Royal Canadian Mounted Police. Nor were there doctors, nurses, or government teachers.

Because all supplies for the post came by shipment from the South, if we ever forgot a particular item in the yearly requisition, we either went without or improvised. Our first child, for example, was seven weeks old at shiptime in 1937, and we overlooked that he might need shoes before next shiptime. An Eskimo woman, Nellie, kindly made him finely sewn, waterproof, white sealskin boots, which I kept clean by washing in soapy water and hanging up to dry. But they always became stiff. So Nellie taught me how to chew the shoes to soften and reshape them. Our Eskimo friends, seeing him totter around in his new boots, called him Iksharyout-naputna — the little, little minister.

I joined my husband in 1933 at Eskimo Point, and we were together there for almost eleven years. Then he was made archdeacon of Aklavik, which required a move to that northwestern settlement. There he continued his work with the Eskimos as well as with Whites and Loucheux Indians. In 1950, as bishop, he expanded his work to the far corners of the Arctic, which occupied him till his death.

We shared in many of the experiences that he has recorded in this book. He often spoke to me of his desire to set down in print what he perceived to be a short but vital paragraph in the history of the North. In my attempt to put together this book, I have thought of it as "unfinished business" that I know my husband had intended to undertake during his retirement years. The book is his; he is the author and the speaker. I have simply arranged the content of his notes into a readable format and put them into a loose sequence of events.

I have attempted to match the photographs to circumstances and, to the best of my knowledge, all the photographs are his. Donald took literally thousands of photos, processing them in a small improvised dark-room in our home. One difficulty lay in keeping the solutions at the correct temperature, as the room was unheated when the door was closed to seal out light. These were our fun times and many an Eskimo would sit and watch the mysteries and magic of photography.

I have to thank many who encouraged and inspired me to tackle the work: Peter Durham Dodd, Ken Bell, Audrey Livernois, and my children, David, Rosemary, and Valerie, for the initial planning and sustained support when it all seemed so overwhelming and difficult. Thanks also to Chris Holloway, who dared to sort and untangle the subject matter with me; to the typists, especially my first, Kathleen Rolfe, whose enthusiasm kept me tenacious in my purpose to persevere. Finally, my gratitude extends to Richard Mitchener, who with professional expertise completed with me the organization and the final editing.

Further acknowledgement and thanks for grants must go to the Canada Council and to the Georgina Houses Foundation. The Public Archives of Canada have carefully preserved many of the early black-and-white negatives. The special care needed to produce negatives for reproduction was undertaken by Ken Bell, to whom I am sincerely grateful.

PART ONE
THE FIRST
YEARS

CHAPTER ONE
INITIATION

JOURNEY INTO THE UNKNOWN

Mile 214 on the Hudson's Bay Railway, August 1926. An immaculately dressed policeman came striding along the railroad track. Every fourth or fifth step, his khaki handkerchief flicked off dust stirred by the slight breeze of this very warm summer day. So this was the North! But it was much too warm. And the forest still surrounded us. At what point would it diminish to the tundra? Later on, I would realize that this was really a banana belt compared to places I would yet experience in the real North. Behind me were school and college years and, now a newly ordained deacon twenty-three years old, I was setting forth into the Arctic, to the Keewatin area in the Northwest Territories.

My fellow passengers and I were traveling northeast on the then unfinished Hudson's Bay line; it would be five more years before it reached its terminus at Churchill, on the bay. I too was headed for Churchill but by way of York Factory, almost two hundred miles to the south. My ultimate destination was Eskimo Point, a seasonal camp for Eskimos with a handful of buildings, some two hundred miles farther north of Churchill on the edge of Hudson Bay.

The train went no farther than Mile 214, and a gasoline-powered rail jitney conveyed me to Mile 333, the end of steel. This last stretch of rail was obviously very makeshift; the jitney occasionally ran over lengths of rail line suspended over gullies deep enough in some places for a person to walk. From Mile 333 I traveled by canoe to Nelson and York Factory. The mosquitoes were voracious. I had never imagined that such hordes of these insects could exist in such a land. We crossed portages at river rapids, I ate dried moose meat for the first time (tough as leather and hard on the teeth), and we finally arrived at the old fort in York Factory. In the fort's munitions magazine I saw discarded wrappings from charges for guns, with the bygone year of 1817 marked on them. Here was a piece of Canadian history.

A small motorboat from Churchill was there to meet me and my companions, a Cree Indian and the Hudson's Bay Company (HBC) manager (or "factor," as they called them). We set out in the stillness of a really hot day, and having cleared the muddy reaches of the Severn River we entered the surprising calm of Hudson Bay. The water was a flat calm, and I was warned to pray that it would last! The boat leaked like a sieve but would have to serve until a replacement arrived. For three successive nights we stopped offshore to ensure that we were in a position of safety should a sudden storm overtake us at sea. Nor was it very reassuring, on approaching Fort Churchill, to learn that we should be ready to jump overboard when we neared Merry Rock, where a river current of some twenty knots meets incoming swells from Hudson Bay to produce great waves. But we had no problems that day. The Churchill River is a great body of water with tides that leave mud flats on its north side. Here were the mission and the HBC buildings. I was glad to meet the missionary-in-charge and his wife, with whom I stayed. From the time we left Mile 214, the journey had taken almost a week.

The following days at Churchill were anything but idle, for I had to pull down two buildings and remove the nails from the lumber to make it ready for transport north to Eskimo Point. Almost immediately I set to work with the aid of several Chipewyan Indians. This was a new adventure for me, dismantling a large building. A week later, the HBC factor arrived from the post (some three miles away) and informed me that the building I was working on was the wrong one. All I could do was to throw the lumber into the shell of the building and begin anew on those that had once been the barracks of the RCMP. It seemed at the time to be a waste of time and effort, but at least I learned how a building is put together. The boards came off one by one, to be passed to one of the Indians, who pulled out and saved the nails. I later prized these above all my possessions, as nails for rebuilding at Eskimo Point were omitted from my annual supply list.

At last the two buildings were merely piles of lumber, and the HBC factor kindly agreed to lend me a scow upon which to pile it to await the arrival of the schooner. The lumber was piled high in the scow, the windows and doors resting against the pile of wood. In the sandy cove near our work, the tides were such that for one hour only, at full tide, was it possible to navigate a boat. In the centre of the cove was a huge rock some seven or eight feet high. The motorboat that was to tow our scow across to the anchorage site arrived at the critical moment. Lines were made fast and the scow started to move, but a wind sprang up and swung her sideways right on top of the rock, and there one end stuck fast. The motorboat had to leave with the tide before damage was done to her hull. There was my month's work floating on the scow, which was slowly rising at one end as the tide lowered the other, to settle it upon the mud. There was little sleep for me that night, but oh, how I prayed, for out there was my future home, the only protection I would have from the elements of the Arctic.

A kindly Indian had kept watch all night, but there was nothing anyone could do. Morning saw the scow settled at almost a 45-degree angle, with one end on the rock; the next tide lifted it and then set it down on the mud again at low tide. But with the next rising tide a few hours later, it was free and could then be towed across the river. My prayers had truly been answered, for not a single stick of wood had been lost.

The schooner *Fort Nelson* arrived. She was a squat vessel built of timber, and her capacity was not very great; her work during the summer was to distribute the annual supplies that were brought into Fort Churchill and Chesterfield on the steamer *Nascopie*. We set sail for Eskimo Point, a voyage of some two hundred miles, the deck loaded half-way up the mast with barrels of oil, sacks of coal, canoes, and dogs. That night I went to bed with the reassuring comment from the district manager, "When you wake up in the morning, you'll look out and see Eskimo Point."

My thankful heart was to receive a shock, however, for I was roughly awakened about three in the morning by someone shaking me. As my eyes became accustomed to the gloom I could see a man whose shaking hands held a pair of trousers into which he was vainly trying to put one foot, as he shouted, "Get up! Get up! We're sinking! Get up!" Then in a flash I remembered I was on the northbound schooner, and I heard the roar of inrushing water below the cabin. Belowdecks a solid stream of water poured into the boat at the stern, while from above came the rhythmic sound of the pumps as the crew tried to keep the boat from sinking. My thoughts flew to the cargo; on board was everything I owned, but more important were the supplies and materials for building a mission house, church, and furniture, together with food and fuel for an entire year. We poured coal from sacks, smeared the sacks heavily with lard, and stuffed them into the hole where the stern post had torn loose. With wood from packing cases we nailed over the hole. The repairs held, and by midmorning we were still afloat.

Two days later the little schooner was towed into harbour by whaleboat. As we drew near the shore I saw before me a flat, unbroken line of land little higher than the sea itself. This was to be my home for the next seventeen years.

ESKIMO POINT

When the anchor dropped, against a background of conical skin tents I saw old men with long, flowing hair, smiling, wrinkled and seamed faces, clad in caribou skins so stained with dirt and grease that many of them looked the colour of the earth. They stooped slightly forward as they walked, as if to help themselves along, yet with the dignity and ease of men sure of themselves.

As I was firmly entrenched in my proper British perspective, the women I saw appeared to be far from clean, with matted, straggly hair and greasy clothes made of animal hide, and yet each had a very attractive smile as she shook hands. With a shrug of the shoulders, they would hitch the babes they carried on their backs so that little brown eyes might peep over the mothers' shoulders with shy intent to shake hands. Most of the youngsters howled when they saw me, for they were not used to white men, especially ones with glasses. One two-year-old, copper-coloured little girl shyly regarded me with her big brown eyes and at last stretched forth her chubby hand, leaned out, and in a flash touched mine before quickly withdrawing into the haven of the pouch on her mother's back. I saw the little naked body so close to the bare back of her mother and thought how comfortable and warm such a nest must be in the rigours of winter.

The young men and boys grouped together by themselves, and their appearance gave me quite a surprise. Almost without exception they were dressed in striped jersey sweaters, their hair closely cropped and cut squarely in front above the eyes. Sweaters and pants alike were store goods, and only on their feet did they wear traditional garb — sealskin or caribou-skin boots. These surely could not be Eskimos! Thus the first of my stereotype images began to crumble.

I enlisted the help of some of the men and boys, and when at last we had finished unloading the lumber and supplies and had carried them to the building site, there just remained the task of building my house and church and making all the furniture. Again the Eskimos helped. Despite my not having any previous training in carpentry, and even though the Eskimos could speak no English and I could not yet speak Inuktitut, the house was ready for occupation in a few weeks.

When I arrived, it was early August. By the time the house was basically completed and I had managed to assemble a few pieces of furniture, the fall season was fast coming to a close. Some weeks later, when winter arrived, I at last saw

Visiting families inside their igloos during winter to talk, preach the gospel, and conduct services. The children, always eager, loved to sing choruses and hear stories.

25

the Eskimo of the picture books and of my dreams. The men, who had been out hunting, arrived running by the side of their dog teams wearing rich chocolate-brown caribou-skin clothes; often wielding whips with a forty-five-foot lash, they would neatly clip a lazy animal and send him to renewed efforts with a yelp.

These were the men of the Arctic wastes, the men I would come to know intimately in their snow houses as, seated beside their fur-clad wives, they heard time and again the old story of the love of God for men and women. Often as they sat on the snow bench and listened, a little brown naked body, secure in the warmth of its mother's pouch in her coat, would suddenly poke out its head and bounce up and down to the tune of hymns or, suddenly spying a strange white man, would raise a howl. Then it would be pacified only after it had been swung around inside the coat and fed. The older children would sit on the fur-covered snow bench clad in

In the spring, Eskimos from an area of 50,000 square miles would congregate at Eskimo Point, a traditional summer camping site. School was taught every morning, and evening classes were held twice a week.

suits of caribou fur, hoods up, and warming hands inside their attigis (inner coats) against their bare bodies.

My first winter was settling in; routines were establishing themselves, and I was beginning to build a rapport with these people whom I had come to teach but who, I learned, had so much to teach me.

SCHOOL IS IN

Broadly speaking, in our civilization we think of children learning a set curriculum irrespective of what they will do later in life. The Eskimo had a very different idea. He was very practical and thought that his children needed to know whatever there was in life that they were likely to encounter so that they would be able to handle any situation with ease. Therefore, children were instructed by their parents as soon as they were able to understand and were educated in many ways.

In summer at Eskimo Point, Donald often visited families in their tents, to talk and teach. In this tent Ooyopek (at right) and her children, of mixed descent, lived with her old mother and father. Ooyopek's mother (at left) is already fast asleep in her sleeping skins.

From east to west across the entire Arctic, mission stations were established at places where food was abundant and therefore where Eskimos would congregate. At such places HBC supply ships would call once a year with supplies for their posts and for the missions and with trade goods for the Eskimos, who eagerly awaited this annual event. With his congregation right at hand, the missionary taught in church and schoolroom, often with both adults and children in the classes. And though the educational process may have been arduous for both teacher and student, at least initially, I can state without much fear of contradiction that as the result of mission teaching, almost all Eskimos today can read and write in their own language — Inuktitut.

At Eskimo Point they congregated from an area of roughly forty or fifty thousand square miles, including almost all the Caribou Eskimos known as the Padlimiut. I taught these local Eskimos during the Sunday services and twice a week in the evenings, and also held school every morning for two or more hours. Often in the afternoon I visited in their tents. I had to start basically from scratch in practically all subjects, including religion (beginning with the Creation) and the three Rs, and teach all things upwards from there. But before I could get their interest, I had to instil a desire to learn. On the whole they tended to be slow learners, but that was probably because their value system considered my kind of education unimportant. They didn't stick to reading or listening for long, perhaps because they were so used to a free and easy life. Everything seemed to need endless repetition before it would sink in. But there were individual children who were quick to respond.

The people also seemed to lack strong religious ideas. Some of their superstitions persisted, although for many the superstitions and taboos had nearly disappeared in the sense of their being unimportant in their lives, and for them the result appeared to be apathy. This was generally true of the Padlimiut. But there were certainly many other Eskimos (see chapter 6) who were still beset by many superstitions. Several of the Padlimiut had Bibles, but they found it difficult to use these because many of their words were in a different dialect and they couldn't understand all they read. So I really had to teach more than read with them, and I had to obtain all the words from the natives themselves. Because of their language teaching, however, I got on very well with learning

Inuktitut; when I went away out on the trail, so to speak, I found that I was able to hold services in the igloos and institute family prayers. But even so, they were teaching me more than I was teaching them in those early days and months.

There were times in our classes when I tried to use lantern slides, but the Eskimos did not readily understand them. They couldn't at first fathom what a picture was. I used to show them photographs of themselves, yet they couldn't recognize anything. For them the photographs were just a series of black lines or blotches. But soon they understood and became used to them, and I would often use pictures from magazines and tell them of snakes, monkeys, camels, and the like. It might be a surprise to know that they had a name for the elephant. Apparently at one time they had heard of one that was in the ice away to the north. The animal was likely a mammoth, and though these people had not actually seen it, as with everything else that happens in this country, what one knows they all know.

The first time I held school in my house, in a confined space of some twelve by sixteen feet, the little room was crowded and therefore hot, and soon the aroma of ancient caribou skin, putrid seal oil, and unwashed bodies persuaded me to let the fire out and open wide the window. Despite a thirty-below temperature outside and a fair wind, there was no appreciable change made in either problem. At least part of the solution had to lie in soap and water. Therefore I put out a basin of water, a towel, and a comb, ready for use before each session. This became a highlight of "school," with grandmothers and children alike assisting each other to delouse themselves. Gradually, week by week, the pupils became much cleaner and enjoyed being so.

The introduction of soap for washing was a new idea, for in the past soap had been used as a perfume, kept in a ditty box and not associated with water. My pupils enjoyed using our Turkish towels, which they thought to be much nicer to use than a chunk of caribou skin, which usually served as a wiper for dirty hands.

White people's customs were very strange, generally, to the Eskimos; we even washed dishes! It wasn't uncommon to see an Eskimo housewife lick a plate or cup to remove grease and then wipe it on her clothes. Winifred, my wife, once made tea for some girls and later found the cups shiny and clean, well licked and polished with their head scarves.

A little girl scrubs with soap and water before school classes begin. School lessons, like church sermons, were as much about hygiene and health as about religion and the three Rs.

Then there was little Amoutilik, who found a big puddle outside the mission house and decided she too would do some washing. Removing her socks she began to imitate rubbing on a scrub board in the puddle, but the sudden appearance of her mother effectively ended the wash session.

Washing at fifty degrees below zero is really not a pleasure even if there were hot or warm water. Eskimo women take great care and are most dainty when they cut up meat or use their ulus, their half-moon-shaped "women's knives," to flense raw skins. With almost exaggerated care they hold the skin or meat with their thumb and fingertips, their hand held as far away from the body as is practical, and with sleeves pushed well back up the arms and out of the way of blood and grease, they proceed with their work. The less blood or grease on one's hands, the easier to get them clean, and an available caribou or bird skin makes a good towel. No one washes hands in snow unless it's very necessary, because the snow may be at a temperature well below zero.

Teaching school was quite obviously not the only time when the Eskimos could learn. My sermons were often about the folly of spitting on the floor, about the ravages of tuberculosis or influenza and the way in which both diseases spread, and with advice as to how best to combat them. It was always a source of pride when I saw an Eskimo bring an empty can to church to spit in when he had a cold rather than using the floor or the open window or the stove top. This was quite an achievement, in my opinion. Gradually one saw cleaner faces, combed hair, repaired or new clothing neatly sewn (tradition and taboos forbade sewing caribou skins while a person was at the coast). So hygiene and the three Rs went hand in hand in schooling.

The curriculum of a mission school (and there is actually no need to specify it as a "mission" school, because there were simply no other schools) was simple. We didn't expect nor hope to train Eskimo children to speak English; to whom would they speak? The trader? He spoke pidgin Eskimo and always used someone to interpret for him if he couldn't manage himself. It's generally useless to learn a language unless you can constantly use it. Simple hygiene, how to add, subtract and do small sums in arithmetic, all of which would help in trading, were the basics given to every child. To read and write in their own language helped them to read their Bibles and prayer books as well as to communicate with people far off, and some history and general knowledge of the world gave the children and adults a bit of background of a life apart from their own. In this way was laid the foundation of education; for what the children learned, though limited, would be helpful to them in the days and years to come. Such schools as this actually set the foundation for the government educational system.

As years went by, students became cleaner and much more studious, as formal education became important to many Eskimos.

Perhaps I should add that in the western Arctic there had been for some years residential schools run by the church for Indian and Eskimo children, but mostly these were in a very different environment from that of the little mission schools run by the local missionaries in the very isolated parts of the Arctic.

Seventeen years after my first arrival in the Arctic, after a visit to Baker Lake in the early 1940s, I wrote the following about its mission school: "The little wriggling bodies lounging on the mission house floor, with sometimes wildly waving legs and outthrust heads peering intently at the board in the mission house kitchen, were the winter contingent. The summer school was held in the church. There were some sixteen to twenty children present, and an older girl of about sixteen years had taken over. She played a recording on a gramophone. It was in English and as the sounds came, so did the young people try hard to mimic those most difficult sounds which made up the English language. They could count, they could read, and they thoroughly enjoyed the

English services, which they could read from the Bible and prayer book and so join in the services with white people." Later, these same children attended Fort Churchill Vocational and High School and did very well.

Of the mission activities throughout my years at Eskimo Point, to the Eskimos school was a high priority. Women could and did attend school, though not always, of course, for there was work to be done at home. The men often weren't able, for they were off to the edge of the ice floes in spring or to the nets in summer. The Padlimiut were, by time-honoured custom, at the coast and at Eskimo Point only for the summer period; the rest of the year they were inland hunting and trapping. For these reasons I decided to hold school in the evenings except for the days when we had service.

We started with a small class of some six or seven men. The going seemed slow and I often had the notion that I would never get anywhere. Arithmetic was easy; they soon understood it. But the English writing was hard to do, and the English language wasn't easily grasped.

The Padlimiut, unlike the Eskimos of Baffin Island, count in tens, so that one can easily count to great numbers. The Baffin Island people, on the other hand, count by twenties or, as they say, by people. Twenty ("arwatc") is really one person's fingers and toes combined, but if you count nineteen you say, "Tedlemarooktoot sittamaroohtohlo attousvalo," which is twice five and twice four plus one. This clumsy method has resulted in the Baffin Islanders learning English numbers and using them in church services and often in general conversation. The Padlimiut still use their own method of counting.

I felt that I never got anywhere on one score, and that was teaching the men the English language. Apart from the repetition of English words during lessons, I never heard one speak a word of English. I always spoke in Inuktitut, so there was really little need for them to speak English to me. Then one day I asked an Eskimo for an article which I knew he had; I was certain he knew what I meant, but he pretended not to understand. Neither Inuktitut nor English was of any avail; he just wouldn't comprehend and the matter was left. A couple of days later he came to me and asked for something, so I feigned not to know what he wanted. He tried in Inuktitut, then to my surprise in perfect English, but of

33

course I still pretended not to understand. Suddenly he burst out, "You understood last week! Why can't you understand today?" to which I replied, "You didn't understand yesterday, and so I can't understand today. That's all right, isn't it?" He burst out laughing and we had no more difficulties with language, and from then on he often understood what I said in English. His sense of humour, as with almost all other Eskimos, was great.

Long Sam was a night-school pupil. He traveled with me year after year. We were often away from home for three months at a time on the trail. We spoke only in Inuktitut, and I used to feel discouraged because Sam never seemed to have profited from my English teaching. In 1943, when I left Eskimo Point and went to Aklavik in the western Arctic — and it was three or four years before I was at Eskimo Point again — I heard of the Eskimos traveling to Churchill to trade, which apparently they did by dog team in winter. But, I protested, how could they trade? No one can speak Inuktitut

Sam, Donald's friend, guide, and travel companion for many years. Sam and his wife, Hikoliak, were the first among the Eskimo Point native community to embrace Christianity. Donald's first winter dogsled trip was with Sam.

down there. "Oh," said my informant, "that's easy. Long Sam interpreted." "Oh no," I replied, "he can't speak English." "Can't he?" was the reply. "He speaks as well as you do. Sam isn't the only one who understands but who won't speak English."

The main concentration of teaching took place in late springtime, while on my winter visitations it was more on a family, or one-to-one, basis. In the spring as many as 350 people would gather at the settlement of Eskimo Point. It was a busy time of great activity that continued through the summer. Winter at Eskimo Point, however, was very different for me, especially in the seven long years before my wife arrived at the mission.

THE GREAT SILENCE

To travel or to live on the great Barren Lands, the wastes of the Arctic, is to know and hear a silence you can almost feel. In winter the sea ice moves and cracks with the rise and fall of the tide. The west coast of Hudson Bay is shallow, full of reefs, rocks, and boulders. When the great weight of frozen sea ice settles on this uneven sea bed it cracks with ear-splitting reports and sharp explosions. Silence can be intense and uncanny in the middle of winter, but it isn't only the silence of the North. For in the early days when southerners went north to live, they lived alone, and then they really found silence — a silence not only physical, but often one that became a silence within their minds, especially after several years in the Arctic.

The silence within your home when you were alone could be broken by the crackling or shifting of coal burning in the grate. Outside, the howling wind — sixty, seventy, even eighty miles an hour — swept past the house, wreathing and mantling everything in snow. Sometimes when that impenetrable wall of white enveloped the building, then you experienced the absolute knowledge of being alone — knowing that no one is able to interfere with your solitude. Only occasionally above the roar of the storm, from a distance, the mournful sound of a howling dog would break the eeriness.

The perpetual chores and the sameness of daily living in the Arctic emphasized the need for something to break the monotony of the cooking, washing up, making bed — the same old things day after day. There eventually had to come the time when you took control, to make your own way of life meaningful. You felt the need to set aside certain times when you simply had to work, or otherwise you would find that you didn't want to work at all. You had to plan, to discipline yourself. If, for instance, you didn't go to bed on time, you very soon found that you were reading far into the night, ultimately turning night into day. These were outward things, but they often indicated the subconscious state of your mind.

There was also the realization that somewhere outside, far, far away, there was a world still going on, and that you weren't there. Sometimes you even doubted if your loved ones could be living the way of life that you had enjoyed with them at one time, because it just didn't seem to exist. It seemed to be a fantasy world, and one from which you felt to be so removed and remote.

The veil of silence of Arctic isolation was sometimes broken by the arrival of a traveler by dog team. Perhaps it was the one winter mail delivery. You poured it out onto the floor — three or four bags of it! Only letters, because parcels were too heavy to haul. Then you pawed through the pile in search of the one with the latest date. You would hurriedly read it to see that all was well with your loved ones. You read and read letter after letter, until you seemed to be unable to contain more. Then wearily you dropped off to sleep, still dreaming of home. When perhaps three or four days later you reread the letters, you would find things in them that you never knew were there. As you read, you would stack the letters until there was a great pile ready to be answered.

Afterwards there would be time to think. Then would come the homesickness and the recall of things going on in the outside world, with the temptation to question the futility of living in a place where you were set apart from outside experiences and people. There was a lot of time for such thoughts, especially when storms attacked the Barrens and it was impossible to go outside for a week or more on end.

Then it was that you had to face the question of whether or not life is worthwhile in the North. You questioned what you were doing. Am I justified in doing this with my life? Am I big enough to take it? Here was the challenge. Am I able to do things for myself? Will I give in? It was then that the realization of the presence of God became very, very real in my life, and I found Him very close to me. I began to reassess my values about Him. I reexamined the value of the things I taught. Were they practical? Would they work? When you find that there are things to question, you build a new set of values to take the place of old ones. It's the challenge of this sort of thinking that weeds out the weak from the strong for people in northern isolation. The weak leave. The strong remain to become even more whole within themselves than they were before.

There were times when I was anxious to talk with someone, and there was no one. Then I would put a record on the gramophone (in later times the radio took its place), and I would play it often, listening to the sound of other people's voices.

Isolation makes you feel these things. And when, as often happens, you find that you haven't enough coal in the bin to burn, you're forced virtually to risk your life. You must go out in the midst of a storm in which you can't see a foot in front of yourself. You know that no one will know if you get lost, and no one will look for you until it's too late. You tie a rope onto the outside of the door handle and, holding to the end of the rope, you grope your way through the white, whirling snow to the coal pile, find the sack of coal, tie the rope around its middle, and then fight your way back to the door. With all your might, you drag that sack of coal into the doorway and so into the house.

These were times when I realized how puny humans are compared with God and the powers of nature, a realization of how easy it is for a man to get lost, to perish, and an appreciation of how wonderful it is that the Eskimo people have learned to live in an incredibly harsh environment such as this and survive. And they didn't even have houses — nothing but snow and skins! You gain a deeper sense of respect for them as you recognize what they face unflinchingly, and you acknowledge what a great race of people they are. So the loneliness of the Eskimo, and the aloneness, leave a mark on a man who lives in the North, and it stays on him forever.

Incidentally, the sun never shone as high or as warmly as on the day that my wife arrived.

SPRING CLEANUP AND SHIPTIME

Spring is a wonderful time in the Arctic. The sun actually begins to feel warm and the snow starts to melt. The sun's rays reflect off igloos, but they also bear down on their roofs,

Winifred (Win).

which can collapse on the unwary at this time of year. Well do I recall a three o'clock morning visit from a family who burst into our home laughing hard because the igloo roof had fallen on top of them in bed. The next day they erected a tent shelter within the igloo as the final stage before moving out. Some igloos were not rebuilt and after the long winter there would be pieces of skin, bones, old clothing, and all sorts of things left outside, so the whole area looked and smelled filthy at the coming of the thaw. No one worried about pollution or runoff into the lakes. It was easy just to move to another spot.

The coming of the white man did anything but set a better example. Garbage littered the ground outside their houses and often around the whole settlement as well — tin cans and other assorted rubbish, mostly blown around in storms. Down on the sea ice an accumulation of the year's garbage made ugly landmarks; these were places to be avoided when going out on the sea ice to collect the melted snow which, paradoxically, gave the purest drinking water in the world.

It therefore became necessary that a cleanup of the settlement be organized to prevent outbreaks of epidemic disease. Such a disaster had happened many years previously, when sewage thrown out of the front door of a house made for impossible conditions on the Labrador coast and people became ill with influenza in the spring; it wiped out a large number of the population. This also happened at Eskimo Point the year following our move to Aklavik. The people were struck with a serious "strep throat" infection similar to diphtheria which was caused, it was thought, by drinking water from the lakes that we had earlier condemned as unsafe.

All the garbage would therefore be cleaned up around the settlement and dumped on the sea ice nearby. And then one day, when the wind happens to be offshore and the tides are high, the sea floats the ice away from the shore, taking with it the piles of garbage and depositing them far out to sea. Spring — and the mosquitoes — have come.

From miles and miles around Eskimos would converge on Eskimo Point, for generations a traditional summer camp site. While the ice was still in the bay, we would spot the first sled (often with a sail up) coming in over the sea ice in early May. Soon games, drum dancing, school, and church

Raising summer's tent is the task of women and young boys. First a tripod is set up, then the other tent poles, which form the skeleton, are leaned against it. When all the poles are in place, a skin line is wound round and round the top, binding the poles tightly together. Then the tent cover is raised over the framework, a difficult job that men often help with. The tent cover is made of heavy caribou hides, and in winter it serves as the roof of the igloo.

activities as well as hunting filled the long hours of daylight. Summer was a time of preparation and replenishment. There were caribou meat and arctic char to be preserved, moss to be gathered for fuel, tents to be repaired, skins to be dried and softened for clothing, tobacco to be prepared. And in a season of plenty there was always lots of feasting. But perhaps the highlight of the summer was shiptime.

Shiptime is a magic word in the Arctic, the event of the year, an occasion long anticipated and one it was always a relief to have finished. Of course, shiptime isn't confined to the arrival of the steamer or schooner; there are hours and hours of preparation for this visit, even though the visit with all the officials may last anywhere from only one day to three or four. There is the painting and decorating, inside as well as outside of the buildings. The stone-lined paths have to be

A Padlimiut skin tent for summer and fall use. Meat dries in strips on a pole in front. Occasionally two families lived together in such a tent.

Women cooking outside a double tent, using moss as fuel. A ring of piled moss surrounds them at right. The woman in front is sitting on a sled. The tent at left is made of caribou skin; that at right is canvas.

Summer is a time of plenty, when preparation must be made for the months of dearth to come. The process of food preservation by dehydration is an old story to the Eskimos. Flat slices of meat would be laid out on rocks or on skins to dry in the sun. (The dark blebs on the skin are scars from warble-fly larvae, which hatched and grew under the hide.) When it is thoroughly dried the meat will be in hard, leathery strips, which will be stored for use in winter. This meat was considered a great delicacy.

straightened and the stones whitewashed. Not a piece of paper, skin, or old tin can must mar the cleanliness of the scene. Police, trader, missionary — each has vied with the other to present a clean settlement with a general scouring and cleanup of the whole place, including the Eskimo camps.

With no radio it was impossible to tell when the supply ship would arrive, and at some posts a reward was given to the first person to see the ship come over the horizon. That

Bent over from both the weight of her load and the distance she has carried it, a sturdy Eskimo wife manages a smile as she nears home with a huge load of moss for fuel. She folds her long, baggy hood forward over her forehead to bear most of the load. Sometimes a very young baby will be secured on the top.

person would run into the post with a cry of "Oomiaryooak!" and then everyone would rush out to sight "the big boat." The flags were hoisted, a last-minute cleanup took place in the houses and, all arrayed in best suits or uniforms, everyone who possibly could crowded onto one small boat which, very heavily laden, bravely pushed its way out to meet the larger vessel. This was the only time anyone ever saw the mounted policeman in uniform, and it was only when an official inspector arrived that he turned out in scarlet. Inspection over, however, blue jeans soon became the order of the day again.

A favourite springtime activity for women and children — picking cranberry leaves for use as "tobacco." Preparation involved chopping or crumbling the leaves, then parching and quickly toasting them in a hot frying pan. The Eskimos smoked this as is or they would mix it with "shag," seamen's tobacco, if it was available. Here a youngster shows mother where she has missed a few leaves.

Almost before the anchor hit the water, the hatches were uncovered, slings dropped into the hold, and the freight started to land on the deck. No one from the shore would be really uninterested; it had been a full year since they had received mail, and each eagerly took his packages. (In early days what were known as skip boxes were filled with mail and addressed to each person, but later, mail bags took their place. I remember one man having twenty-six large mail bags full, containing letters, parcels, daily newspapers for a year, and magazines and books innumerable.)

Always the scene was a riot of activity. There was the mail, the freight, people passing from one post to another,

Shiptime. Eskimo men, women, and children unload goods and supplies from the schooner Fort Severn, *anchored offshore at Eskimo Point during the first week of July, as soon as the ice has moved out.*

others going on furlough, the checking of supplies, the counting of numberless bags of coal, the rush to get cases counted to see that the ship had unloaded all your supplies. It was a rendezvous on board when everyone would be dressed in his or her best, but only for a short time, because the freight took precedence.

Soon your best suit would be discarded for overalls. The packages of personal-delivery letters the captain gave you from the post down the coast would be gone and in its place you held a checklist. When the whaleboats and canoes — hired from the Eskimos and packed with the whole settlement — arrived at the side of the ship, the Eskimos would clamber aboard and watch the unloading. The Eskimo owners of the boats would stack the freight, and boats once fully loaded set off for shore. This called for a hasty return to shore by the whites, who had to scramble onto the load laden with mail, the checklist in hand and possibly nursing a gift of some fresh fruits and vegetables — the first in a year.

Ashore the cases were thrown onto the beach, where some men and all the women, with scattered children, toiled up and down the beach carrying goods to ground above the

45

high-tide mark. As the Eskimos carried the boxes, bales, bundles, crates, cases, and drums up the beach, you had to try to read the address, number, and weight of each item, to see if it was yours and onto which pile it should go, to be carried to your house as soon as the tide turned, when it would no longer be possible to unload. At low tide, the goods were taken to the store or warehouses, and in between checking, the owners tried to get mail read and short notes scribbled to those at home to say that all was well. Shiptime was a rat race.

With freight bills signed, and tired out from spending the night writing letters or stumbling on the beach searching for lost cases, you were glad to see the boat go. Usually some of your spare time had gone towards a visit to the dentist or doctor, for if you didn't see one then (and you were lucky if there was one on board), you certainly wouldn't see one again for another year. But before the last farewells, there were the bales of fur to be loaded; these were the real reason the ship sailed north every year.

A medium-sized schooner delivered our goods to Eskimo Point every year, because the shallow, reefy western shoreline of Hudson Bay prevented navigation by larger vessels. (I never actually saw the only ship that served the whole eastern arctic, the *Nascopie*, though I was in the Arctic for years.) The HBC at Eskimo Point had an outstation at Padley, and all supplies were transported there by canoe. Not all cargoes arrived safely at shore on our coast. One small boat partly full of water was loaded with freight consisting mostly of sacks of sugar and a few violins, ordered in for trade. The water flowed to the stern and soaked everything there, and when the sugar was unloaded a sticky fluid oozed down the backs of the Eskimos. Later the fiddles fell apart because the water had loosened the glue holding them together. Such risks were part of Arctic life and made life interesting.

Occasionally there were some queer incoming and outgoing loads. Once, in the early days of aviation, there was an airplane with a crumpled wing; the two wings were taken from the fuselage and the whole thing hoisted on board the schooner to be taken south. Then there is the story of the three pigs, Arctic style. Each of the managers of three HBC posts had decided to order in a pig, fatten it, and slaughter it in the fall. Shipping the pigs north would be no problem; they would live on the incoming schooner with some chickens and a cow or two. There were no refrigerators in those days, and so fresh meat remained on the hoof and was butchered as needed. The cut-up meat kept well in the cold atmosphere. But back to the pigs.

Lofty Stewart, at Chesterfield, thought it was fitting that the pig scheduled for Eskimo Point should be colourful, and so he instructed the clerk to choose the largest pig and daub every colour of house paint that he could find over the pig's body. This work of art was duly done, and everyone turned out to see the handiwork. One of the three pigs was for Baker Lake, leaving a second smaller one and the large pig with the kaleidoscope treatment.

The schooner was ready to sail and the crate readied for its gaily coloured passenger, but the pig had grown. The crate was found to be too small, and so the unpainted pig had to be taken south and the coloured one left with the originator of the idea, who didn't appreciate the art work when the time came for slaughtering. The one that did go south to Eskimo Point broke out of the crate anyway, and a merry chase ensued all over the vessel before he was again caged.

In a country with no lumber, housing the live pig at the post presented a problem. It was solved by making a pen with bags of coal. Holes between the bags provided toeholds for the Eskimos and enabled them to climb up and look over the top of the bags. The pig every so often would give a deep grunt and instantly the onlooker would let go in astonishment and fall backwards to the ground. Of such are Arctic memories made.

The aftermath of shiptime — when at last all crates, boxes, bundles, and other items were stacked away — was when the whole settlement would converge on the store, where the people would be paid for their help in unloading. Soon it would be time to go back out on the land, and with debts secured the Eskimos would leave by boat or canoe or even walk to their winter campsites. Shiptime was over and for a full twelve months the routine of Arctic life would be settled as it had been for years.

One fall we faced a serious dilemma. The supply schooner was late, for August and September had passed and it was now October. Ice had formed into a great barrier around the shore and slushy slub ice had formed on the sea, making the passage of boats difficult. Still the schooner had not come, and we counted the bags of coal in the settlement. There was only enough for one dwelling place for six weeks or at the most for two months. Food also was low, but there was enough to last for one man until after Christmas. We decided that the trader should have priority because he had goods in the store that the Eskimos would need. The rest of us should make our way south, but how? There was no snow for sleds, and boats were simply out of the question. Then one day the cry "Oomiaryooak!" went up as an Eskimo finally saw the schooner and called from house to house with the good news.

That was a tough shiptime, leaving us battered and bruised after slipping, falling, and sitting down on boulders rough with ice. Most of the Eskimos had long before left for inland, and only three were left on the post, so we had little help. I carried my ten tons of coal in bags of 112 pounds each over that quarter-mile trip from the unloading point to our mission house, plus several tons of supplies. But we were safe from cold and hunger and thankful that we would again be able to face the winter.

CHAPTER TWO
ON THE BARREN LANDS

SLED TRIP WITH SAM

My first trip by sled took place during my first winter in the North, in 1927. It began at 5 A.M. when the alarm rang. I arose and padded to the window, then peered through double-paned glass to see what the weather was like. The deep blue-black of a lovely clear sky dotted with a myriad of stars met my eyes. It was not yet light, but there was a fine glow illuminating the eastern horizon. Breakfast, a last check that I had all I'd need, and I carried everything outside to the sled. There would be neither stores nor places where forgotten goods could be obtained.

Late in the previous evening I had finished the careful and critical preparation for the trip. Much had been required. The lamp box with two primus lamps, a snow knife, rifle and cartridges, sleeping bag, sleeping skins — all have to be readied, as do the contents of the grub box. This last matter is most important, for in the box go the matches, mugs, knives, forks, spoons, and the like, plus numerous bags containing the food for the trail. Food must be previously cooked, the beans boiled, stew boiled and frozen, then all broken into chunks for easier handling. Each variety is placed into a bag, from which it can be taken and quickly heated with little loss of scarce fuel on the trail. Since the Eskimo camps were scattered miles apart over this vast area of trackless snow — for there are no roads, paths, or trails — visiting from one camp to another may necessitate several days of journeying; preparation, therefore, simply had to be adequate.

Sam had already iced the runners. Together we spread a tarpaulin over the sled, placed on top the caribou skins for use under our sleeping bags and then, starting with the grub box on the front, added the sleeping bags, primus lamp box, and the rest of the gear. We folded the tarp and lashed everything into place.

Sam sorted the long traces for the dog team and harnessed the dogs. He hitched each one to the bridle in front of the sled while the dogs padded around sniffing it and each other. A call to them, a crack of the whip, a shove of the sled, and the team leaped forward. We were off. Soon the post was out of sight. The first furious pace slowed as we crossed firm sea ice and reached the flat, monotonous Barren Lands.

Traveling inland, we passed over hundreds of moss hummocks, or neearkoptuk (resembling heads), that dot the Barrens in many places. They're often so numerous that there's scarcely a foot between them. Little by little the landscape changed. The sled slid onto a flat surface of snow, and our weight caused it to break through the snow crust. This meant we both had to walk. If either of us tried to ride, the sled broke through and bogged down in the crystalline snow beneath. Presently the dogs began to break through also. We slowed from a fast walk to a crawl, with Sam and I just pushing the sled. The temperature was well below zero, but we became so warm that we removed our outer coats, our koolitaks, and just wore our inside coats, our attigis.

Each step became more painful as we advanced. The hard crust tore against our caribou-skin socks, and our shins were soon sore and bleeding. Our backs began to ache from so much bending and pushing. At times the poor dogs were as hard put to travel as we were.

It was almost nightfall when far ahead we saw a small light glowing through the ice window of an igloo. It was a welcome sight, and the spurt put on by the dogs showed that they too had seen it. In the dusk we could see figures appear, and finally at the igloo we shook hands with Sam's family. Everywhere was bustle as the dogs were unharnessed, tethered out and fed, and our gear shuttled into the snow house.

This was my first visit to an inland Eskimo camp. With much interest I ducked down through the igloo's opening and into the porch. The porch jutted out from the igloo and decreased in height as I proceeded forward. I skidded down with bent back, then inched my way forward on hands and knees. I never did learn the almost crablike motion that an Eskimo uses when he slides and slithers along the passage into an igloo.

Entrance to the igloo of Sam's family. Most of the living area is well beneath the surface. A snow porch, used for brushing off clothes and for storage of meat and other goods, juts out from left. The flat roof of the igloo lies beyond view in back of the entrance. Two families shared this igloo, living together in it from the first big snow, which usually fell in November, to the spring thaw, about seven months.

Once through the inner door and into the igloo itself, I was within circular walls fully twenty feet in diameter at the base. The roof was flat, for crossing the top of these snow walls were the long tent poles now used for rafters to support the caribou-skin tent cover, which formed the ceiling. It was white with rime. On one side of the snow wall was a great slab of ice let into the side for a window. Across two semi-circular sections of the igloo were two snow benches built in such a way that they joined at one point. These indicated the igloo was the home of two families.

Near the door stood a bucket and dipper, both made of caribou skin and frozen solid. The frozen carcass of a caribou, solid as stone, was propped up to one side of the door. The only furniture the house could boast was an iron camp stove in the very centre of the igloo. From here a stove pipe went up through the skin roof. Near the stove was a small bundle of willow twigs, the longest of which was ten to twelve inches. This fuel wasn't for heating the great empty space, but just to stew the meat and boil water for tea.

An Eskimo chops up frozen caribou meat with an axe within the entrance to the igloo. Walls of another section of the dwelling appear at far right and left.

I was assigned the privileged sleeping position given a white man, in the middle of Sam's family's snow bench. As soon as it's dark Eskimos retire to bed. After family prayers I slid into my sleeping bag, with a considerable jolt from its coldness. Crawling into a bag that has been left all day in a temperature of fifty below zero is a chilly adventure to say the least, but by curling yourself into a small space when you first creep in, and gradually stretching out by degrees, it's possible to warm the bag with your own body before the bag in turn starts to warm you. Initially, as I slid into the bag, the fur of the inner bag felt silky and very soft against my naked body, if very cold. To be able to stretch my weary back and legs was luxurious. It was then I discovered that the skin on my shins had rubbed off and had bled inside my stockings. I needed no rocking that night, but at about two in the morning I woke to hear a loud cracking on the roof. I wasn't the only one, for Sam woke too and yelled, "Kaneecoonee!" ("Too close!") The loose dog treading on the igloo

The family sleeps together on its snow bench. Sleeping skins are placed on a mattress of willow twigs, so the skins do not rest on the snow. The warmest spot is in the middle, a privileged position, which Donald was assigned.

was warned off. We could hear the crunch of his footsteps as he moved away from the igloo.

The next morning I awoke to find that Sam was up. "Coffee or tea?" he asked. When I requested coffee, he brought me a queer, brown-coloured liquid in an enameled mug. As I sipped I found it almost full of tea leaves, and when I asked Sam about it, he broke into a conciliatory grin. "It's coffee, but I left tea leaves in the kettle when I put the coffee in." Lying in the warmth of my sleeping bag, I ate and drank slowly. The wind howled across the igloo's roof. A real storm had come up, and I was thankful that we'd arrived the day before rather than camping a night between here and home. I dressed and moved onto the floor of the igloo. On my way out to reconnoitre I smiled at a young woman who was carrying in water in a skin bucket.

Outside, it was just a wall of white. Snow driven by the furious onslaught of wind was everywhere. Little mounds

A young maiden carries in fresh water from a hole made in the frozen lake surface. She uses a caribou-skin dipper and a moulded caribou-skin bucket. Both are frozen solid into their forms.

appeared in the porch and grew bigger every moment. Even in the porch the dogs would get up every now and then to remove the load of snow from their backs. They'd then curl up once more, protecting their noses with their big bushy tails.

54

The storm was to last twelve days. Twelve days I spent in that igloo with the two families, whose genuine pleasure mounted as day by day they, my teachers, improved my Inuktitut vocabulary. The storm was so fierce that we were forced to remain indoors. Supplemented by caribou meat, the food we had carried for our journey fed us until there was little left; we kept only a small bit extra on hand for our return journey. And so I realized why it's always wise to carry a month's food for a week or two's trip on the trail.

The Caribou Eskimos assume a peculiar, hunched position when they sit. If a man sits on the edge of his twenty-inch-high snow bench, he'll sometimes let his legs dangle down so that they almost touch the floor. This is done only on the few warmer days when it's perhaps only around the zero mark or a little lower both in and outside the igloo. When it's really cold inside, he squats on the bench, sitting on soft caribou buckskin laid over plaited willow-twig mats normally used to keep the bedding dry from the snow underneath. This way he's certain there will be no contact with snow or ice. He can undo his shoes and perhaps, if he's in his home, slip on another dry, more pliable pair. Feet encased in stockings worn with the fur next to his skin, plus a second pair on the outside with fur facing outwards, the Eskimo is warm, though he may have to tuck the ends of his bell bottomed pants under his legs to stop off a cold draught. With the hood of his parka or attigi, he covers his head and tightens a little more the belt around his coat. In that way no cold air makes its way inside. Hands left outside soon get cold; so, taking his arms out of his sleeves, the man draws them next to his body, where they soon warm up.

I watched Sam as he smoked his pipe, thrusting his right hand through the neck of his inner parka for warmth while he meditatively puffed away. The dangling, open arms of his coat let in the cold. He showed me how to fold them up and tuck the openings under the elbows through the thickness of the coat. An Eskimo can sit and ruminate for hours in this position, often with his legs crossed in front. Smoking silently, he occasionally spits at the wall with amazing accuracy. After all, he has had much practice. If spoken to, he will give only monosyllabic answers unless someone comes in to whom he wishes to talk.

Hikoliak, Sam's wife, also sat on her heels. It's a peculiar stance of Eskimo women, all of whom sit with their heels

In wintertime children play mostly in the igloo; even in fine weather, the intense cold makes it impossible to stay outside for long. Here two children amuse themselves inside their igloo poking holes in the wall.

together yet with their feet spread out, rather like a butterfly. A woman sits that way literally on her feet and can so remain for hours, never moving unless she finds some reason to do so. She too might let her long boots and socks hang from the snow bench. When her hands get cold from sewing, she easily draws them into the front of her coat and warms them against her body.

In wintertime, children mostly play in the igloo. It can well be fifty below zero inside the igloo as well as outside. There's no heat in the dwelling, save for the negligible amount given off by the people themselves, each person giving off the equivalent in heat of a 100-watt light bulb. Sometimes the children cry from the cold, and their little hands sometimes become chapped with chilblains. They stand with their small hands inside miniature parkas, their hoods drawn tightly over their heads, and their runny noses look so sore when they have colds.

Occasionally Hikoliak swung her chubby baby girl from the nest in the pouch of her parka onto her lap to be nursed or set free to explore her surroundings. For a little while Hikoliak could concentrate on the new socks she was making for Sam. Admiringly I watched this little naked mite, with her smooth, coffee-coloured skin and enormous brown eyes, clamber across the rich brown bed skins of caribou. Eskimo babies are very appealing, cuddly bits of humanity and seemingly quite impervious to cold. She captured all my attention when suddenly I saw a big bruise at the base of her spine. About two inches in diameter, it was dusky blue and well defined. It looked as if it were the result of a really hard blow, and I wondered how it could have happened. I felt sure that it must have been the result of an accident. I knew Hikoliak and Sam very well as highly respected people who loved their children. Wondering, I kept silent. Then one day I saw the same spot on an adult, bigger this time and not as well defined, with the edges fading to match the surrounding skin. Later I learned that all Eskimos bear this mark, the Mongolian spot, which appears also in some Indian tribes and the people of Northern Tibet and China.

Now I turned my attention to Hikoliak, busy preparing a caribou skin for sewing. Caribou skins are dry and rather stiff if they have been dried in the sun, and first must be scraped with a steel-bladed scraper. (Before steel arrived, the scapula of caribou or other animals served the purpose.) Hikoliak held the scraper in her right hand with palm facing outwards and forced the scraper across the taut surface of the skin held firmly between her knees and her left hand. This process frees the skin from all subcutaneous tissue and any fat left when the skin was first removed from the animal. She then squirted water evenly over the entire surface, rubbing it into the skin, which she then rolled up and set aside for an hour or so to dampen evenly. She chewed any hard parts to soften them. Next she used a stone scraper to break down the skin fibres, an operation which appreciably stretches and increases the size of the pelt. Following this she took another steel scraper to scrape off the inner skin, leaving material downy soft and creamy white and very pliable. Now she was ready to cut.

Padlimiut women use no patterns, nor do they measure, but they do a remarkably fine job of fitting any garment, even if most of the garments are quite roomy. Hikoliak took her ulu and cut out roughly the shape of one leg for a "sock." She used the first leg as a guide to cut the second one, carefully folded the edges together and firmly marked the seam on the inside of the skin with her teeth. Turning the skin inside out, she trimmed the edges until they exactly matched. She cut out the sole next, and the sock was ready for the final sewing together.

From a pile of dried sinew, she took a fine thread and drew it through her mouth to moisten it, then pulled it through her fingers once or twice before threading the needle. Sewing skins with hair on them, Hikoliak had to poke the hair down between the two edges of the skin with the side of the needle after every three or four stitches. Next she hooked the thread around a finger and drew it tightly. From toe to heel is the rule for sewing socks or boots, and so the last portion she sewed was the leg.

Quite abruptly, Sam said he was hungry. According to custom the master of the house tells his wife when he is hungry. Slipping on her boots, Hikoliak laid aside her sewing, picked up her baby and settled her in the pouch, and set food before us all. First she laid a skin of unhaired caribou and a small handaxe on the bed, then a haunch of frozen caribou meat. Dinner was served. Suddenly struck by another thought, Hikoliak remembered some seal oil, stored from the summertime when the family had been at the bay coast.

An Eskimo woman preparing to sew a caribou-skin inner sock for her husband. She has already prepared the skin and cut out the pattern. She sews with dried sinew, which she first moistens by drawing through her mouth, then stretches, before threading her needle.

When the family is not entertaining a visitor, it's usual for the master of the house to chop at the solidly frozen meat, and with great skill he strikes the same place with every blow. A fine sliver of frozen caribou gradually curls off the haunch. It's so cold and the meat so hard that it's difficult to cut. Dipping the sliver into the oil, father quickly stretches his head forward and into his open mouth pops the meat, with great care not to spill the oil on his coat. (There are no dry cleaners in the Arctic.) Each child chops for himself unless he's too small to do so; then father or mother will chop some for a youngster. Clutching their portions, the children stuff the meat into their mouths and chew before swallowing. Everyone often eats frozen, raw meat and as many as thirteen or fourteen times a day. The meals aren't big but are snacks that provide the internal heat necessary for life.

At last everyone is satisfied and the household resumes its monotonous routine. The children sometimes visit their relatives on the other snow bench to play their simple, time-consuming games. A homemade checkerboard scratched on a wooden box top provides hours of enjoyment. Sometimes an older child or parent cuts out figures of birds or animals from caribou skin, and with a lick on the back of the skin and a slap on the snow wall, the figures stick on contact.

Teesheeootnak, a relative of Sam, who with his wife shared the igloo, was one of the few Padlimiut who were poor hunters. He did much around the camp, however, hauling caribou from caches and doing a dozen other chores around the site. He decided to travel back to Eskimo Point with us. We were late in starting, and so we camped part way home. When the igloo was built for the night and supper was over, we laid out the bed skins and sleeping bags. Teesheeootnak discovered that he had no bag. He merely undid all the strings fastening his garments, took off his pants to use for a pillow and his outside coat for a sleeping bag. Putting his feet into the hood and hauling the skirts of his coat around his neck, he curled into a ball and was soon fast asleep. Since he didn't move in the night, he had a good sleep. Often he and many others of the inland Eskimos sleep out in the open like that.

My first sled trip left me with time for deep introspection about life in the North, about these amazing people, and led me to regard them more and more highly. People able to survive and live as they do are really tough, tougher by far than I. For though I've enjoyed sleeping out in the open air at thirty-five below zero, I've been inside a sleeping bag and thankful for it. But it's also a grim life, even for the Eskimo child who must learn to "take it" and to accept as normal and inevitable many difficult situations, ones that would never be a concern in the warmer South. This lesson starts early in life and carries throughout life itself.

THE MISSIONARY'S MISSION

My primary purpose for being in the North was to minister to the spiritual needs of the people, to share with them the message of Jesus Christ and the offer of His love. Some years after my first sled trip I often made my winter visitations for that purpose with my close Eskimo friend Joseph Yarley, whose story is truly inspirational. But more of him later. I recall one particular journey that we took together in 1941, particularly because of a pot of tea that we shared with a family of Eskimos and the realization that I came to because of it.

The thermometer registered thirty-eight below as Yarley and I lashed our load onto the sled, harnessed the dogs, tied on the bag containing the dog chains, and with a hurried goodbye to Win, set off. Our route lay inland across the flat Barrens. The dogs were cold and anxious to be moving. They rushed across the lake in front of the mission and down onto the sea ice. One of us on each side of the sled's front, we pushed and pulled to keep the nose from hitting ice hummocks that had been thrown up by the boulders lining the shore. Across the flat sea ice we sped, and in ten minutes or so we were across the little bay and mounting the slight rise on the other side. The winter had been cold but with few storms, and so the surface of the snow was fairly smooth.

At midday we came to a small lake and were thankful to be able to sit on the sled for a few moments while sliding over the ice. Reaching the other side, we decided to have our lunch before continuing the trek. From the grub box on the front of the sled, Yarley brought out the vacuum flask and a bag of pilot biscuits. Lunch was quick, for the tea, when once poured out, rapidly cooled and we were fast getting cold.

After untangling the dog traces (a job that had to be done every two hours or so), we traveled on until the sinking sun reminded us that it was time to stop and build a shelter for the night. Yarley began to keep a sharp look out for snow suitable for building an igloo and finally saw a huge drift in the lee of a slight rise. He stopped the dogs. With his snow probe — humorously referred to by men in the North as a "nouk stick," because most Eskimos say "Nouk" ("No")

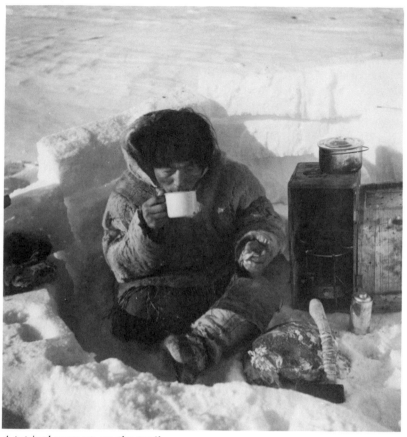

A typical mug-up on the trail.

every time they probe and find the snow unsuitable for building — he tested the snow and pronounced it perfect.

He first described a circle on the surface of the snow, indicating the size of the igloo he intended to build, and then set to work cutting snow blocks. While he was doing this, I busied myself by pegging out the dog chains, unharnessing and chaining the dogs. Then, having unlashed the load, I piled snow against the blocks that Yarley was rapidly putting into place. On the south side of the igloo I then built a porch, and as I finished, Yarley cut a doorway at the base of the igloo, forming an opening into the porch about two feet square. I passed a candle inside to Yarley. As if by magic, a beautiful dome-shaped structure of pale, pale gold suddenly appeared against the dark background of the sky. The outline

The overnight igloo almost ready, Yarley cuts his way out from inside and emerges holding the door, his snow knife clutched in his right hand. The next morning, when Yarley and Donald depart, they will seal the igloo so that any other travelers will find it ready to use should they need it.

of every block showed clearly as the light of the candle filtered through between them — a truly beautiful sight.

Yarley was busy smearing snow into cracks, and now and then I could see his shadow as it moved across the interior of the igloo, appearing and disappearing for all the world like some grotesque dwarf. When he had finished the sleeping bench, I passed in the sleeping skins, which he beat thoroughly one by one and then laid on the sleeping bench. The sleeping bags followed, also beaten in turn, and then the lamp box, grub box, and last of all the coal-oil can. Having set each in its appointed place, Yarley emerged from the doorway and I crawled in. Removing my outside coat, I beat it and laid it at the back of the igloo, but I would later use it to give added protection to my feet against the cold. I next beat off the snow from my clothing and set to work to prepare supper. I lit the two primus stoves, placing on one a kettle filled with snow and on the other the frying pan containing a little snow. As soon as the snow melted, I put into the frying pan several frozen balls made largely of cooked meat, beans, and rice. By the time Yarley came in from feeding the dogs, supper was ready.

He made a vent in the top of the igloo to let out the fumes from the lamps and then beat the snow from his clothes. We sealed the door with two snow blocks, which he had put to one side for this purpose when he made the igloo.

Supper was soon over, and after Bible reading and prayers, we undid and spread out our sleeping bags and soon were fast asleep after the long day.

By six o'clock the next morning we had had breakfast, more Bible reading and prayer, and Yarley opened the door by simply cutting around it with his snow knife and kicking the blocks out into the porch. Taking a small saucepan of water, he went outside to put a coating of ice on the bottom of the runners of the sled so that it would run easily. I pushed the bag containing my sleeping bag into the doorway to keep out the intense cold and then packed away the lamps, kettle, and food. As I finished Yarley came to the door and said that the sled was ready. So with my foot I pushed out the bag blocking the doorway and passed out to him all our camping gear. Together we placed it on the sled, lashing the load tightly. With the dogs harnessed and the igloo carefully sealed so that anyone passing that way would find shelter for the night if they needed it, we were once more on our way.

Towards noon the wind increased until the surface of the snow was covered with rivulets of drift, which has the appearance of steam forced from a pipe onto the ground and then blown this way and that. By the middle of the afternoon the wind was of such force that we could hardly see the lead dog, and the driving particles of snow stung our eyes and faces. But we were only a few miles from the camp to which we were traveling, and we were sure we could arrive before movement became too dangerous. (Often during such drifting, visibility drops to only a foot or two, and even the Eskimos, with their marvelous sense of direction, get lost.)

At about four o'clock in the afternoon the dogs shot off to the right and, peering down, we could just discern fresh sled tracks. In a moment or two we came upon the camp. It wasn't a group of dome-shaped igloos, as one might expect to find, but only six snow porches standing out on the almost

Children love to be the first to find out who has arrived. Like little rabbits they run out to see and then dash back into the igloo to spread the news. Padlimiut igloos are not the dome-shaped structures usually pictured by people in the South. Initially Padlimiut igloos are built on the ground, with almost vertical walls and with flat roofs made by stretching the skin tent cover over the tent poles, which act as rafters. Very quickly successive storms cover these igloos, so that they become virtually underground. After a storm a way must be dug out — hence tunnels and steps lead from the surface to the interior.

flat surface of a large snow drift. Directly behind each, a six-foot snow chimney reared up and beyond each of these I could see a slight hollow, around which stood one or two tall snow blocks. These blocks were placed there to reflect light in through the ice windows of the igloo.

The many tethered dogs had started to howl immediately upon our arrival, and their chorus brought out a man and several children to the doorways. The man, Adgikshaot, came across to us and invited us to stay with him. We accepted, and he went back into his igloo, saying he would return when he had put on his outer coat. Yarley and I at once busied

65

ourselves with the dogs, tethering them in a long line, and then we unlashed the load; our host rejoined us and helped. Caching things that we shouldn't need, we carried our sleeping bags and other gear down three steps into the porch, where the children seized them and rapidly pulled them down the long line of porches ahead of us.

Bending our heads, we followed them, and as we proceeded we bent more and more until last I had to get almost on my knees to get into yet another porch. Here we were met with a blinding eddy of wood smoke, which stung our eyes and made us gasp. It was coming from the cooking porch. On the left was a snow bench about three feet high, upon which burned a fire. Large, flat stones formed the hearth and three square stones made a fireplace on it. Crouching nearby was a woman with streaming eyes and a bad cough. Not waiting to see more, I stumbled forward, almost blinded by the smoke, and was brought up sharply when my head hit the wooden top of a doorway. The door was about thirty inches high, made of wood from boxes, and I had to get on my knees to get through. Yarley and Adgikshaot, however, slid through with the ease of long practice into a porch common to three igloos; the doorways that opened into it were without doors.

Through one of the doorways we followed our host and found ourselves in an igloo almost thirty feet in diameter, with a sleeping bench running down each of two sides. The circular wall was almost vertical and across the top, parallel to each other, were laid twenty or more long poles (used for the tents in summer), and over these was stretched the caribou-skin tent cover. This arrangement explained why no dome had appeared from outside.

Once we had divested ourselves of our outer garments and beaten them, our host's wife, Nedbat, laid on the sleeping bench a haunch of frozen caribou meat and a handaxe. This was merely a "taster." It's hardly necessary to say that she brought in a kettle of boiled black tea and an array of enameled mugs.

Very soon the numbers of children who had entered the igloo on our arrival were supplemented by all the men in camp who, after shaking hands with us, sat on the sleeping bench. Some of them, to make room for others, removed their boots and sat at the back. All, however, took care to leave a space in the centre, upon which, in a short while, was laid a large wooden dish piled high with split, boiled caribou heads. After repeated invitations from our host everyone set to with a will, and soon all that remained was a pile of bones.

By this time it was getting late in the evening. So a young boy was sent to all the other igloos to call the other women and children to a service. In a short while the igloo was packed with men, women, and children of all ages. The body heat from the thirty-odd Eskimos was hardly sufficient to raise the temperature of that igloo even one degree. I watched their intentness as they listened to the lesson and sermon, and within me I felt no doubts just then as to whether or not missionary work is worthwhile. Hearing of a God who loves them and who gave His Son for them means much to a people whose only conception of religion is one of fear and whose everyday life is bound up in a series of taboos, the breaking of which they believe could mean starvation or some other disaster. Not unnaturally, such ideas and beliefs cannot be changed in a year or two, nor indeed would it be advisable that they should be until they can accept the teachings of Christ and live them in their everyday lives. Christianity must mean to them something that can help them and something that they can live before it means anything at all.

After service the people went to their homes to bed, and after family prayers with the two families who lived in our host's igloo, we laid our sleeping bags on the bench and also retired.

Six o'clock found everyone awake, except for one or two of the smaller children. After a breakfast of frozen caribou meat and tea, we joined once more in Bible reading and prayers. Yarley and I sat and talked for a while with our host and then made a visit to several of the other igloos. These were of varying sizes, depending on the number of inhabitants, but in the main were replicas of our host's home. It's during these informal talks that the missionary is able to help the people with any specific problems that might be confronting them. As well, we could give a few words to those who asked for more instruction or advice about hygiene, or provide attention for those in need of medicine or other medical care.

At eleven o'clock we met once more in Adgikshaot's igloo for service and instruction. Then we had dinner and visited some more of the igloos. We held service again at four o'clock and then had supper, said prayers, and went to bed.

Thus ended a typical day in the life of a missionary among the Eskimo camps.

We knew we would see these people later in the year, as they would come to the coast in the spring and spend the summer there. So we set off the next morning to go farther inland. Our visits to other camps were but a repetition of the day already described, and it was nearly two weeks later that we entered a camp where I met some Eskimos who were strangers to me. These were some of the people to whom an Eskimo woman referred when she said, "I feel so unhappy to think that there are many Eskimos living inland who don't know about Jesus." Her words are only too true, but true also of those in other parts of the North and who aren't able to "hear without a preacher." There comes to mind a native who lives at Igloolik. He traveled from among his own people at Southampton Island to teach the people there. He wasn't asked to go. He just went unheralded with his wife and family to share the gospel of love.

But on this particular occasion, Yarley, who also had left his home to share that same gospel, and I were inside a large igloo almost thirty feet in diameter and without heat, except, of course, for that from our bodies and the puppies who kept wandering around the floor looking for something to eat. Here we sat, stranded for several days — two men, two women, two children, Yarley, and myself — squatting on our heels on the sleeping bench with our arms drawn up into our inner coats, backs hunched up, hoods drawn over our heads, moving only now and then to retuck our empty sleeves under our elbows to cut off the draught.

It had been a long while since anyone had spoken, and the glances thrown at the door every so often showed that everyone's thoughts were with the woman in the porch, hoping and hoping that her fuel would last until the kettle boiled and the tea was made. I can just picture her as, huddled against the snow bench, she would thrust willow twigs into the fire's hungry maw, and every time the flame died down, she'd bend and blow until she was red in the face. The embers glowed, and the flickering flame caught the new fuel, throwing her face and figure into sharp relief. I can see the tears as they streamed from reddened eyes and coursed down her dirty, smoke-stained cheeks, leaving furrows of comparatively light brown skin behind them. I can smell the acrid smoke of the willow burned for fuel and can see it billowing

Lighting the fire in the cooking porch to boil the tea kettle. The willow twigs used for fuel give a smoky, flickering fire that has to be tended constantly. In the intense cold, over that weak flame, the kettle may take up to an hour to boil.

into her face before it swirled around and eddied up the snow chimney, to be caught in the onward sweep of the Arctic blizzard, and in a flash to be lost to sight.

I can see that red glow in my mind's eye, yet I stay here, for cold as I am, I'm warmer than in that porch where the fire will boil the kettle but will give almost no heat.

The long tramp home in the dusk and the cold.

What toil that fast-dwindling bundle of twigs represented! Weary, backaching toil — the jumping on the hard snow, the beating apart of lumps that cling to the smaller twigs, the scratching with mitted hands to scrape away the soft, sugar-like snow, and then, one by one, the cutting of the six- to eight-inch-long willow twigs. She would gather these into pitifully small bundles, tie them all together into one heavy load and lift it onto her back. Lastly, there would be the long tramp home in the dusk and the cold, only to arrive knowing that most, if not all, of her labour will go up in smoke before she has even made a cup of tea.

Momentarily, my thoughts jumped to the world "outside," with gas, coal, and electric stoves in every city home. What a far cry from "civilization," to be here in an igloo waiting for tea.

Creak . . . Creak . . . Bang! I awoke with a start from dreams of warm homes in southern climes and saw walls of snow. I felt cold. Ah! Here comes the tea. That dirty, soot-encrusted kettle, which was once shiny bright aluminum — I, with my Eskimo brothers, look upon it almost with affection. My host stirs. A moment ago he seemed like some ancient Buddha, unmoving, as though carved from stone. Now he thrusts arms into his sleeves and places before him a board (once the end of a condensed milk case), and on it his wife sets the tea kettle. With a clatter she arranges a miscellaneous assortment of mugs close by and pours out the tea. An old caribou skin serves as a table cloth, and on it she throws a thigh of frozen caribou meat and a small axe.

"Please eat," requests my host, and I come to life. My hands find their way through the sleeves, I shift my body till I can reach the mug. Frozen meat doesn't have much appeal, and thanking my host I tell him, "Presently," and cling to my mug. It's scalding, but I hardly feel it, my hands are so cold. And as the heat begins to register, I turn the mug around and around in my hands. If there were only some way of warming the backs of my fingers.

I detest boiled tea, but this mug-up is wonderful. As I gulp it down, a warm glow steals over me, and presently I set it down and chop myself a piece of frozen meat from the haunch of caribou. Before I've eaten it, I notice minute crystals of ice forming around the mug. My tea is cold! I drink it up at once, for I remember my hostess has worked for three hours collecting those twigs, almost half an hour carrying them home, and almost an hour boiling the kettle. Four hours' work. And the result? One kettle of hot tea, gone cold in two or three minutes.

FALL HUNTING ON THE BARRENS

Fall was a crucial season for the Caribou Eskimos, for their survival depended on the success of the hunt. Every year at this time the caribou migrated southward toward the coniferous forests for the winter, following time-honoured routes. These trails were well known to the Eskimos, who placed their inland camps at strategic points, often at river crossings.

For a long while I had wanted to join some of my Padlimiut friends on one of their hunts in the interior. We'd be late for the mass migrations, but we hoped to find smaller bands of caribou. With great excitement and anticipation of the journey I had packed carefully the previous night, making sure my movie camera and films were accessible on short notice. I slept as a child does on Christmas Eve and awoke very early. I made final packing arrangements and readied the dog team and sled. It was seven o'clock and not yet sunrise.

In a few moments, however, the sun rose over the bank of grey cloud that always hangs over the open water of the sea when the temperature is below freezing. Immediately the greyness of the sky and snow changed; the sky became a glorious blue and the land, with its powdery covering of snow, an almost pure white. Joe and Jimmy (two native police constables), Sam and I were off on a caribou hunt. The lakes had been frozen for several days but still showed dark, ice-free patches here and there. We gave these open water areas wide berth, because ice around them was almost certain to be unsafe for crossing. The dogs, so eager to get off at the start, trotted along at a brisk pace. We crossed one lake after another and made good time.

We stopped for tea at noon but were soon off again. Dropping down a fifteen-foot river bank, we saw two ptarmigan, our first sign of wildlife. Ptarmigan are very trusting birds — foolish, some would say — for they will allow anyone to approach as close as ten feet without taking flight. Today these two would provide our supper. We traveled until four o'clock, arriving at a spot where several stones stood on end at right angles to the edge of a lake. These indicate good fishing grounds and where generations of Eskimos had fished. Seldom, if ever, will an Eskimo try to fish elsewhere if one of these places is nearby. Here we decided to camp for the night.

While we settled in, Joe dashed off to jig for fish through the ice. I could see him as I cleaned and prepared the ptarmigan for supper. Squatting motionless on the ice, his right arm alone moved up and down slowly as he jigged. Joe was perfectly silhouetted against a most glorious sunset, with colours ranging from lemon to light green, crimson to gold, all reflected on the glare-ice surface of the lake. By seven-thirty we had cleaned up the tent, spread out the sleeping skins and our sleeping bags, and after prayer and Bible reading settled down for the night.

The next morning we found breakfast ready, a big kettle of tea and a pile of bannock, courtesy of Joe. Breakfast in bed on the trail is a great luxury, especially when the tent's inner walls are white with frost in the candlelight, as they were that morning. We were off before seven-thirty; the sun wasn't yet over the horizon. A lake on the tundra or a hill very occasionally relieved the monotony of traveling the Bar-

*Arloo's camp in early fall, too early to make an igloo. The main
residence, a skin tent, is at right. A cooking lean-to sits left. Another tent
lies beyond the photo's view.*

rens, until at last we reached a fair-sized lake and old Arloo's
camp.

Arloo, an old man with five grown sons, lived in camp
with two of them. Two caribou-skin tents were on the side
of a low rise, and in front of these a small semi-circular ring
of long willow twigs had been erected by the women. Inside
this windbreak the earth had been worn and packed hard
from much use. In the very centre was a small depression
surrounded by stones where a fire was burning, sending voluminous smoke eddying and swirling into the faces of the two
women and three children who periodically fed it fuel. Burning willow twigs have a habit of going out, and so those who
tend the fire must bend down from time to time and blow
the embers to a flame. It's small wonder that their eyes
become red-rimmed and their faces blackened. Arloo and one
of his sons invited us to his tent for tea. Upon an old piece
of deerskin was a haunch of caribou, frozen of course, and
close by it two knives. One of the younger women brought

in the tea, set out some mugs, and everyone helped himself.

Arloo's wife, an old, wrinkled and white-haired woman, sat beside him on the bed skins and smoked her pipe, passing it every now and then to her husband. Both were angakoks — shamans or conjurors. This old couple, with their sons' families, had tramped at the end of summer over forty miles inland to this campsite, carrying everything they owned, including the two tents, on their backs.

As I sat and talked with Arloo and his wife — and while she filled her pipe from my pouch — I was able to study an Eskimo candle and candlestick. This consisted of an up-ended rock about six inches tall and four inches square, placed on a lightly hollowed, flat rock base. On the base were several pieces of rendered caribou fat, each piece having in front of it a small mound of charred moss wick. When the moss was lit it melted the fat to provide light, which reflected off the upright stone in the middle. From time to time the fat had to be moved forward to ensure a good supply of fuel for the wick. All Caribou Eskimos used these in the days before the coming of the white man.

We declined Arloo's pressing invitations to stay the night and decided we'd push on and later make camp. Sam was well ahead of us, and we'd lost sight of him. He knew this country like a book, but Joe and Jimmy had never before been this far inland. We continued, however, in the general direction in which we'd been traveling and came to a long lake, at the end of which we saw Sam's dog team. There was no sign of Sam, but just as we stopped he appeared, carrying over his shoulder a haunch of venison. Thus we had fresh caribou for supper.

The next morning we picked up the remainder of Sam's caribou and scanned the horizon hoping that more were nearby, but to no avail. Just before noon we reached another "fish lake." Joe, who was ahead, stopped close to some open water, and even before we caught up with him he'd begun to jig. As I put the kettle on to boil, I heard a shout. Joe had landed a fish, a nice lake trout almost two feet long. He tried his luck again for a minute or two before coming back for tea. Tea over, Sam and Jimmy, who wouldn't be outdone, also tried their hands at jigging. Joe took a place close to shore, cut a hole and patiently sat down to jig. Almost at once he landed something and, running over, I saw the tail of another fish whisk around under the hole in the ice, then

*Leaving Eskimo Point in fall, one of Arloo's granddaughters carries a
sleeping puppy in her shawl. They are heading inland to their winter
campsite, some forty miles away. In summer and fall, Eskimos might
wear cotton or woollen clothing bought from the HBC post. "Store-
bought" clothing was entirely unsatisfactory in the severe winters,
however, when the Eskimos would all wear their traditional, homemade
caribou-skin clothes.*

swish, he landed it. A cry of disappointment from Sam made us run to him. He'd broken his line, and a huge fish had taken it as a souvenir. It must have been large, for his line was made of plaited sinew. Joe at once started to jig to see if he could catch the big one.

Looking down into the crystal clear water, I could easily see the white ivory block the hook was attached to swinging slowly around in the water, the piece of skin (from the belly of a fish) which was attached to the hook trailing behind. Patience is needed when jigging, for the fisherman has to sit and watch his hook, and the second he sees a fish take it, he has to move it upwards. Standing beside Joe, I suddenly saw a pink-tinged tail flash across the hole. Quicker than the eye could see, Joe hauled upwards and THUMP, a beautifully coloured lake trout was twisting and turning on the ice. Fried lake trout made a nice supper that night, after which we sat and talked.

Joe, an Aivilingmiut (a tribe from the north who hunt sea mammals for food), told us of how they hunt whales, both the "white whale" (porpoise) and the beluga, as well as larger whales. The talk drifted to bears, and Jimmy told of a little cub that he had when he was a boy. He tied it in the tent when he went to bed and in the middle of the night was aroused from sleep by a sharp pain in his head. The little cub was biting him. He thought it was a good joke, though he admitted that he moved the cub to a safer place.

Joe told us how a polar bear kills and eats a walrus. He said the Eskimos often watched it happen: When the bear spies a herd of walrus on an ice pan, it takes up a large chunk of ice and claws off the edges and corners until it has fashioned a rough ball about two feet in diameter. Rising on its hind feet, it carries the ice ball in its front paws, keeping well behind the ice hummocks until it's as close to the herd as it can get. Singling out a young animal, it rushes forward, and as the walrus plunges into the water the bear throws its missile and hits the head of its victim. The bear continues its rush, plunges in after the stunned walrus, and catches it in its forepaws; then, gripping its hind feet on the ice, the bear pulls the walrus backwards.

Joe then asked us how we thought it skinned the prize. (A walrus hide is an inch thick or more; indeed, walrus hide is cut into twenty-seven thicknesses when it's used for commercial purposes.) Here is his explanation. The bear uses one of his huge canine teeth, or fangs, to rip through the walrus's belly from throat to tail. Then it strips the skin away from both sides and around from the back, but leaves the fat on the carcass. Polar bears seldom eat the meat, but gorge themselves on the fat. Foxes usually take care of the rest of the kill.

Joe then related a couple of stories from Baffin Island. An angakok who had no wife had his eye on a young girl, but she wouldn't have anything to do with him. So he danced around her tent a few times, with the result that she developed a limp, and because no one else would have her, she finally became the angakok's wife.

The second story was of the Toonooeet. Apparently all Eskimos tell of the race of tall blonde giants who wouldn't fight, but who were able to erect huge slabs of stone, which today would require the strength of four or more men to move.

After Joe's stories we settled down for the evening. Next morning, as we pushed farther inland, the snow covering appeared to be much lighter, allowing us to see flocks of thirty or forty ptarmigan, well camouflaged in their winter plumage of white, sitting on the snow in the lee of the land and along the edges of lakes. Then we saw the fresh tracks of four caribou. Always on the lookout for them, we traveled through willow bushes and tiny spruce trees about a foot high, which grew around the lake edges. A few miles farther, we came across trees fifteen feet or so tall, and it was near a bluff of these that we again camped for the night. After tying up the dogs, Sam climbed the hill at the back of our camp. From there he spied four caribou feeding close by, and we soon dispatched them.

We awakened the next morning to the sound of flapping canvas, for the tent was bellying in and out with the gusts of a strong wind. It was a cold day. Later Joe and I decided to drive the dogs into a small bay, where we would be more or less protected from the wind, and make some tea. We erected the tent with one pole and held down the sides with rocks so that it was, to all intents and purposes, a bell tent. Then Joe picked up a fair-sized boulder, held it high over his head and with all his might brought it down on the six-inch-thick lake ice, cracking the surface for a yard around. Where the stone had hit, the ice was splintered into hundreds of little pieces. Repeating this process several times, he soon made a hole from which we took water for our tea. This generations-old method of making holes in the ice was useful for making fishing holes as well.

Joe gave me a haunch of caribou meat and went off to "spy." I soon had the primus stove lit. Thoughtlessly I left the dogs, still on their long traces, lying down about six feet from the tent while I went to call Joe for tea. I had moved only a few paces when I turned and saw a yelping and snarling mass of dogs, each intent on biting the unfortunate one beneath. The lowest in the mêlée was doing his best to defend the caribou meat that he'd filched from the tent. Running back, I picked up a whip and used the butt end indiscriminately to drive off the dogs to the accompaniment of many yelps. The meat was little the worse for wear.

I turned to see Joe descending the hill, and he was putting his telescope into its bag. He'd seen Sam and Jimmy some distance off carrying caribou over their shoulders, so he then took his team to meet them. After sharing our coffee, we took down the tent and lashed the caribou onto Joe's sled and were off once more. The wind had dropped almost entirely. Joe now took the lead. There was little fear of losing the trail here, for he had a shoeing of oak wood on his sled runners; whenever he passed over rocks or rough ice they left a trail of fine shavings to mark his progress. Sam's runners were of iron, and often one would envy the other for the particular shoeing which he himself didn't have. Sam's sled was faster on the ice or crossing rocks, but the other two sleds slid along more easily on the land. Navigating a twenty-foot sled and a dog team with twenty-foot traces between a mass of boulders and open water and along a narrow strip of ice three feet wide is no easy task, especially if there are many turns, and twice I put my foot through ice, wetting my deerskin boots. They immediately froze with a coating of ice, however, and my feet didn't actually get wet.

Reaching lakes once more, we pitched our camp by the side of a high hill, from the top of which was a magnificent panorama. Almost the whole of the surrounding country was frozen water and appeared like a vast sea with a few scattered islets dotting its surface. The ice reflected the colours of the sunset, making an unforgettable picture of the Barren Lands. The snow-covered slopes of the distant hills seemed to make colour richer in comparison with their bluish whiteness. Soon after our midday stop we saw two figures on the horizon. Out came the telescopes, and we soon recognized Pingakaryoo and Shee-etaluk, two natives from Eskimo Point. We waited until we saw them coming our way and then went on slowly to allow them to catch up with us.

We set off across a bay, and the poor dogs had a hard time of it. When the ice was about one-half inch thick, there had been a north wind that had first caused it to split up and then had driven it into this bay, where it had frozen with the sharp edges pointing upwards. Both Joe and Jimmy left trails of splintered wood over this surface, and looking back from the top of the bank we could see the other two teams also leaving dark trails behind them.

It was early when we camped, so before supper Shee-etaluk and Pingakaryoo decided to mud their sleds. Knife in hand, Pingakaryoo wandered around until amost at once he found suitable "mud." This material, which can be found almost anywhere in the North, consists bascially of decomposed lichens and mosses. There are several kinds, some being better for use in early winter, and others when the temperature is very cold. No substance has yet been found that's as light and runs as easily over the snow in the cold winter as this mud. During spring when the sun causes the mud to drop off, steel is used, though it isn't by any means as good as the bone shoeing that was used by the Eskimos prior to the coming of the white man.

Pingakaryoo used his axe to remove a frozen layer of this material, leaving a hole about four inches deep and twenty inches wide. The excavated soil was then cut up until it resembled the consistency of pastry before it's rolled out. Gathering this into a bag, he carried it to the lake and dumped it by the water hole. Making a depression in the centre of the mud, much as cement is mixed, he poured water into it. With his hands he mixed mud and water, rubbing the mixture between his palms until he'd broken up every lump. He added a little more water to make it bind, then made a ball about three inches in diameter. This he carried to his upturned sled, broke the ball in two, and applied half to each side of the runner starting at the nose of the sled. With his thumbs on top and his fingers down the side of the sled, he moulded this material until he had a flat, two-inch-thick surface on top, with about a half-inch overlapping the width of the runner on each side. A few feet away Shee-etaluk was doing the same thing. As can be imagined, it's a cold job,

Shee-etaluk applying "mud" to the bare iron shoeing of his sled. The mud was made from a soil material consisting mainly of decomposed mosses and lichens, mixed with water. It was moulded onto the runners, left to freeze, planed smooth, then coated with a thin layer of ice. This slick surface allowed the sled to run easily over the Arctic snow and ice. Re-icing occurred at regular intervals.

especially when done in winter with the thermometer at forty degrees below zero or more; then it's not uncommon to freeze both hands. Pingakaryoo and Shee-etaluk mudded their sleds in an incredibly short time and left them to freeze overnight.

We left camp before these two, leaving them to plane and ice the frozen runners of their sleds. An Eskimo plane resembles an ordinary wood plane, with a piece of iron for a cutter.

After the mud has been planed, the runners are iced. Taking a mugful of water and retaining it in his mouth until required, the Eskimo squirts it onto a piece of bearskin, held cupped in the hand. (Bearskin is water repellent and won't become soggy and freeze.) With swift movements, he smooths on several applications of water which immediately freezes, to build up a thin, even ice surface on the runners. The sled is now ready and will slip along easily until the ice wears off, which necessitates another stop to repeat the procedure.

About two o'clock the next day, the dogs suddenly pricked up their ears and made off at right angles to our trail. Jumping onto the sled and swaying from side to side over the uneven ground, Sam and I bumped up and down and held on as well as we could. Suspecting caribou, we managed to stop the team, which Sam left in my charge while he dashed up the hill with his telescope. Without even using it he signaled: Caribou! He motioned for me to come, and there across the ridge were about a dozen caribou, the does lying down and the bucks standing by to keep guard.

A caribou herd stands, wary, in the distance while a dog team, linked by fan-hitched traces, waits for their master on the hunt.

We arrived back at the sled just as Joe and Jimmy came up. Then all was rush and bustle as we cached the goods in a pile and tied up the dogs. When all was done we gathered up cartridges and rifles, together with my movie camera; filming the caribou was the real purpose of my participation in the hunt. Joe, the oldest, went ahead with Sam next, then Jimmy and I followed. Making a detour to get within better range, we walked in line, Joe nearest to the caribou, with each of us as close as possible in a direct line on his right. Walking this way, we would appear as only one person if the caribou were to become suspicious.

Presently Joe dropped to his knees and crept forward carrying his rifle. We also did the same, and I began to chuckle, for the whole affair was reminiscent of the games of Cowboys and Indians I played when I was a boy — the four of us creeping along, hugging the ground as closely as possible. We stopped when Joe stopped and moved when he did. It wasn't very easy to crawl with a rifle in one hand and a movie camera in the other; I couldn't allow the camera to touch the ground, or snow might have gotten into the lens. Occasionally I'd be prodded in the back by the muzzle of Jimmy's rifle, when he was watching the caribou and the rest of us had stopped. (I learned afterwards that the rifle was loaded! Had I known then, I might not have felt quite the same kind of excitement.)

One of the big bucks lifted his head and looked our way, then a doe stood up with a characteristic jerky movement. They were very uneasy by this time, and Joe said we might as well shoot. He waited first for me to shoot a few feet of film, then they began to fire. The caribou were two or three hundred yards away, however, and only two were shot as the whole band swung around and off along a ridge, with the old bucks circling back to make sure the does were all right. Suddenly the two animals dropped. The rest immediately turned and fled.

We then split up, with Jimmy and I following the three big bucks while the others followed the rest of the herd and later began to cache their kills or skin and cut up the carcasses needed for immediate consumption. I'd hoped to film a close-up of the bucks. Jimmy and I pursued them for about a quarter-mile, shooting until we had only one shell between us, while the three caribou were making for distant pastures faster than we could follow. As we made our way back to

An Eskimo hunter pulls the skin from the legs of a caribou prior to skinning the rest of the carcass. Skin from the legs is the most durable of all; it doesn't shed and is very tough. It is used for mittens and outer boots.

camp we saw three other dead caribou on the skyline, their heads pointing to the heavens and their horns driven into the earth to anchor them there. These had been cached to be used later in the winter. The upturned heads would make good landmarks when the bodies became covered with snow.

Loading the sled for the return journey after a successful caribou hunt. Primus lamp, pilot biscuits, tea, and other small items will be loaded into the open grub box in the foreground.

Back at camp we found that Joe was busy harnessing his dogs before setting off to bring in caribou to feed them and ourselves. No dogs howled that night, for they'd had their fill.

We woke early the next day and by midmorning, with heavy loads, we were well on our way toward home and knew we were now within twenty miles of the coast and twenty miles south of Eskimo Point. Keeping to a chain of lakes, we made our way to the bank of a river along which we traveled, all the way experiencing great difficulties with the terrain. Then at last there was a place where a tiny stream emptied into the river, and over this cascade of ice we pushed and shoved our sleds. We soon left the river, with the beauty and hazards of its rapids and winding course, far behind.

On the last morning we arose knowing that we had only a short journey home and hoped to arrive some time around midday. A south wind was blowing, and the weather was clear and much warmer; indeed, it was so mild that there was water on top of the ice, and our boots became wet in a short time. Although wet boots meant cold feet, we didn't mind because we were confident we could reach home that night.

Nearing the coast our little stream wound through a plain covered with sedges about two feet high waving in the wind like fields of wheat on the prairies. Often we lost sight of the dogs struggling before us, while we pushed on the sleds with all our might. Then we reached a hill, from the top of which we could see the buildings of the post, at a distance of about five miles. Little snow was on the ground, and there were no lakes, so we continued to push our sleds over the rough tundra for the remainder of the journey. It took us three and a half hours to cover those five miles. For the last quarter-mile we traveled through a blinding snowstorm, but what a joy when the dogs at last could quicken their pace, and we were home!

Joseph Yarley.

CHAPTER THREE
JOSEPH YARLEY, A CHRISTIAN MAN

My knowledge of Joseph Yarley starts on the coast of southern Baffin Island where, in the summer of 1909, the young Eskimo teenager, clad in dirty skin garments, was playing on the rocky shore. Sewn on and hanging from the back of his coat was a weasel skin, an amulet given to him by the angakok to ensure that he would have cunning skills as a hunter when he grew up. Sewn securely to the breast of his skin jacket was a small bag containing the heart of an animal, a charm to prolong his life. His father was off hunting in a kayak and his mother was scraping sealskins on the rocks when the lad spied a ship. It was bigger than any he had ever seen. He ran to his friends shouting, "Killee! Killee! Oomiaryooak!" ("Come out to see this great ship.") When the anchor dropped, a small boat was lowered. Soon four white men stepped ashore. Little Yarley shyly hung back behind the Eskimo men but near enough to hear one of the white men begin to speak in, wonder of all wonders, Inuktitut. The speaker was a man with a white beard, whom the boy soon came to know as Okaoyuk, "the good talker," Dr. Edmund Peck.

The white men had brought all kinds of supplies. Soon they were busy unloading lumber, boxes, crates, and bales. No time was lost in erecting a small mission house. The ship left in a few days' time, taking Dr. Peck but leaving the two missionaries behind to begin their work, the first step of which was to learn the Inuktitut language. Daily the young men and boys sat on the floor of the mission house listening and learning to read and write in their own language. There wasn't much room, but always crowding to the front was the young boy who had first seen the ship, Yarley. Time passed, and it was a year or two before he came to know and love Jesus Christ and to accept Him as Saviour.

Over the years there arose discernible and marked distinctions in the dress of the people: the angakoks still wore belts, amulets, and charms, while the Christians, who no longer feared the spirits, abandoned all taboos and outward forms for the appeasement of the spirits.

At Lake Harbour a tall young man named Archibald Fleming (later the first bishop of the Arctic) singled out the young Yarley and invited him to be a sled boy, and together they set off by dog team to visit many distant camps where the people had never heard the gospel. No compass was used; only Yarley's knowledge and love to guide them.

Together they traveled on some of the longest sled journeys ever made, traveling for weeks behind the dogs, day by day running by the side of the sled, night after night building igloos, always seeking out some Eskimo camp nestled in a sheltered nook from the winter gales.

On the return trip home from one of those journeys, Fleming was running ahead of the dogs to encourage them. It was in the midst of a storm so bad that it was impossible to see more than a few feet ahead, with the driven snow stinging their cheeks and faces like little daggers. The dogs bent their heads before the fury of the wind and followed in Fleming's footsteps, while behind, Yarley was guiding the sled. Just as they were rounding a point before coming into the settlement at Lake Harbour, Yarley remembered a place of open water ahead where it never froze. Suddenly he wondered: Would Mr. Fleming remember it? Stopping the dogs he rushed forward to find that Fleming had already fallen through the thin ice into the water. To pull him out was difficult, for Yarley was a small man, but at last Yarley succeeded. Rubbing Fleming down, Yarley himself warmed him in his own sleeping bag. Quickly he built an igloo and later took Fleming to the mission station. Since Yarley had saved Fleming's life, it's understandable that from then on they always traveled together.

After Fleming's second term of service, he went South on furlough and did not return. The years passed at Lake Harbour, at times without a missionary, but those young men who in earlier days had eagerly listened to the message in the small mission house took the service every Sunday. Now skilled hunters in the community, they were men to whom the people looked to provide food. They became leaders not only in material things, but also in things spiritual. In the igloos, kneeling on the skin-covered sleeping bench, each family would have prayers night and morning. Their Bibles, now bound into translated volumes, became well worn and dirty as the men read and their families listened with eager expectancy, Joseph Yarley's family of two adopted children among them.

Long before, the HBC had established a post at Lake Harbour, and whenever the yearly supply ship arrived, everyone gathered to see who was on board. To the delight of all, and Joseph Yarley especially, who should they see on the deck one particular year but Fleming, now an archdeacon. What joy for Yarley and those who had known Fleming so long ago. What joy to listen to him greet them in church, and at the end to hear him suddenly make an appeal to his old students by saying, "We need a volunteer to go to Baker Lake. Someone is needed to help the missionary there. Is there anyone who will go?" Immediately after the service one of the young men, Pudlo, volunteered and the next day he and his wife boarded the ship and sailed to a part of the Arctic where they were strangers. Years later, Archdeacon Fleming again visited Lake Harbour and called for a volunteer to go to a new mission on the western shore of Hudson Bay. Joseph Yarley hesitated. He felt God had called him, but he really didn't want to leave his life where he was; and yet, if God was calling him, who was he to say no? After the service he consulted his wife and then told the archdeacon that he and his family would go to Eskimo Point.

Several weeks later the boat brought them to a country quite unlike their own and to a people who laughed at him, who weren't ready to accept him as one of themselves. They called him "Okamiut," the man from the other side, and while they listened to his words, they didn't believe what he said. There were many shamans among them who still kept people in terrible fear. Yarley would tell them not to be afraid, for God was greater than all the spirits. In their homes, in his quiet way, he would read his Bible to them. He would teach them how to read; he would explain to them the love of God. He was only one small man, and often things must have seemed almost hopeless; but God was with him, and the impact that he made was slow but sure.

Later Yarley moved seventy miles north of Eskimo Point

to build and maintain a mission outstation at Tavanne. During one winter the snow blocks of his igloo began to settle until the igloo became so low and uncomfortable that Yarley had to cut off the top section in order to replace it with new snow blocks, to increase its height. His only son — born to him in this new land — thought it great fun to run around on top of the wall of the exposed igloo. Faster and faster he sped on the inward-sloping surface until suddenly he slipped. He tried to save himself but fell onto the hard snow bench underneath. At first it was thought that the youngster had only broken his ribs but gradually, day by day, his condition worsened. His father, who adored him, prayed that the boy would get better, but Yarley's only son died.

It was some time later that one of the Eskimos spoke to me about Yarley: "We did not believe Yarley. He told us that God loved us. He would tell us this repeatedly, but we had seen many terrible things happen and just did not believe. Then Yarley's little boy fell down and hurt himself, and we knew how much Yarley loved him. We were sure he would not say that God loved him still, because his boy was sick. When he said the same thing after the little boy died, then we *knew* that God loves us, and because we had seen that Yarley could love God in spite of what happened, we love God too."

PART TWO
RECALLING
THE ECHOES

Inside her igloo Kownuk, carrying her son, scrapes frost from the window. The window is a block of fresh-water ice split from the frozen surface of a lake. Horizontal spruce poles support the caribou-hide roof, which serves in summer as the tent cover.

CHAPTER FOUR
INSIGHTS TO
THE PADLIMIUT

SETTING THE STAGE

I'm not convinced that God had habitation in mind for the North when He set the world spinning on its axis and thereby created two eternally frozen lands. Today we know that the two polar regions haven't always been quite so frozen, for there seems to be ample evidence of warmer climates at one time. Thousands of years ago, perhaps when the Arctic was a bit warmer, Eskimos first came into the Canadian North from Asia by way of Bering Strait or simply by walking over the frozen Arctic Ocean during the glacial period that ended here some nine or ten thousand years ago. They carried little with them, but simply used the few resources that were available in nature. Over countless generations they found and perfected the most appropriate means of adapting the northern environment to their use and survival. But Arctic resources for a hunting people are scarce, and the land could never support large numbers of people. So the Eskimos kept their population low and spread out over the land and the frozen sea. And they survived this land of ice and snow. To understand Eskimo life as it was requires that we understand just how limited their resources were.

Besides food, the two most valuable resources to the Eskimos, paradoxically, *are* the ice and snow, which can just as easily mean death as well as survival. Eskimos had to understand the dangers of the ice as well as the possibilities it offered. An Eskimo can tell you a lot about ice — that freshwater ice differs from sea ice, that the former freezes at a higher temperature than salt-water ice, but that it fractures quickly and its sharp cutting edge is hard on boats and canoes, though it does make excellent windows for igloos. It's dangerous to walk on ice close to moving water or rapids or where an area isn't completely frozen over; such ice may be thin and a trap to the careless.

Sea ice, when it first freezes, is known as rubber ice. It will bend and conform to the surface of the water beneath, and waves can move it up and down in folds. This ice will give under pressure much the same as a taut sheet of cloth will give in one place if you force your finger down onto it. It takes a sudden sharp downward thrust to break its surface. Eskimos living at the coast learn to walk on rubber ice without taking their feet from its surface, slithering their feet along, taking rhythmic, fan-shaped sweeps. An Eskimo can hunt on this ice, but it's dangerous, and he takes his life literally in his feet and must rely on good judgment and common sense. If he breaks through, there is no one to help him out.

Within a few days, however, the rubber ice will become firm enough to walk on safely, while new rubber ice forms farther out to sea at what's called the floe edge. Beyond this area, large or small blocks of ice float at the whim of wind and tide. Hunting at the floe edge is usually good, but there's always the constant danger of the ice moving off due to a higher tide than usual or a sudden offshore wind.

There are places in the Arctic where the tides cause the ice to act like an elevator or lift-lock. This happens where large and almost vertical rocks rise from the water's edge. At high tide the floating ice rises to the level of the shelf of ice attached to the rock face. As the tide recedes the floating ice drops, leaving a vertical wall of ice attached to the rock face as high as the rise and fall of the tide. Should a traveler arrive at such an ice face and want to get ashore, he just sits and waits for full tide (perhaps four or five hours) and then drives his team onto the ledge adhering to the wall; or conversely, he waits on top of the ledge for the sea ice to rise until it's possible to get onto the main floating surface.

Great bodies of ice in Hudson Bay and all Arctic waters move slowly from shore to shore according to the pressure of the wind and tides. The great icebergs of the High Arctic are never seen in Hudson Bay. They come from the glaciers of Baffin Island or Greenland and move into the Arctic or Atlantic oceans with the currents.

To the Eskimo, ice in the Arctic is a power he must reckon with and respect, but which he uses as a resource for survival.

Ice is found only on water surfaces, but snow is everywhere, and it's always there. You can't ever really get away

94

from it; it permeates almost every aspect of life in the North. You walk on it, you live in it, you build with it, you melt it and drink it. The Eskimo language has some thirty-two words to describe it: granular, powdered, drifting, hard-packed, just right for igloos, too solid for houses, so hard a sled leaves no mark on it, and so on.

Snow in more southern climes is light; it's soft and white, with deep blue shadows. In the North it lies clean and white and beautiful on the land, but with a certain mystery. It hides and exposes at the same time. It obscures the few features of the land on the barren tundra, but announces any dark object at great distances. The snow's whiteness blindingly reflects the sun's glare and repels its heat, insulating the ground from any warmth.

A clear day in the snow-covered Arctic is a thing of beauty. There may be a wisp of white swirling like drifting steam, often scudding and curling lazily across the ground surface. But let the wind get up to thirty, forty, or fifty miles an hour, to gale force, then fierce driving winds cut into drifts immovable, resculpt the hardened drifts so solidly that you can break an axe handle in trying to chop it. A man's vision is filled with a relentless, driving mist of white. Tiny particles sting face and eyes. Fine pellets of snow drive into cloth of the finest weave, and only furs without seams can withstand that ferocious onslaught.

Yet that same snow, built in the form of an igloo, is a work of art. Nothing could be more beautiful than an igloo outlined against the pitch black of Arctic night. The perfectly shaped dome of snow is luminous, its every block outlined by gleams of soft light shed from a single candle within. If there's one word that says more about the Arctic than any other, certainly it's the word "snow." *This* is the Arctic; indeed, the snow is a sight I'll always remember and treasure — a snow-covered wilderness inhabited by the Eskimos, the bravest people on earth.

One's imagination is captivated by the thought of these short, furclad people, whose winter homes are domes of snow, who face with equal cheerfulness the bitter winter blasts of Arctic storms and the summer's myriads of mosquitoes and blackflies. Their habitation is no paradise, for their country is wild; nature here is stern and exacting. Down through the ages these people have learned to make much out of very little and have striven and fought and conquered the elements that they might live. They are the Eskimos, the Inuit, "the people."

THE ESKIMOS' NATIVE NEIGHBOURS

Indians also came to North America via Bering Strait, but they didn't stay in the frozen land; they moved into the tree-covered country south of the Arctic. In the Canadian North, the tree line generally marked the division between Eskimo and Indian country. The tree line also marks the division between the Arctic and Subarctic regions.

The tree line is the northernmost extention of the great continental evergreen forest of spruce, pine and fir. West of Hudson Bay the tree line runs roughly in a northwesterly direction from Churchill, Manitoba, past the north side of the great Arctic lakes and onward to the Mackenzie River delta and beyond. But the tree line itself is really undefined on the land; it's a zone perhaps a hundred miles wide, where vast meadows of barren country intersperse with copses or thickets of trees, some of which are little more than two feet tall at their edges, having been sliced off at snow level by the winds. Deeper within a given clump there may be trees as much as twenty or thirty feet tall, and these are excellent for making sled runners or for use as tent poles — if one happens to have such uses in mind. Trees and tundra overlap all through this zone. There is no distinct "line" between forest and barren tundra, and therefore there was no equivalent distinct line separating Indian and Eskimo land. As a result, problems often appeared between the two peoples.

At one time Cree Indians — and subsequently Chipewyans — claimed the country north of Churchill, where occasional clumps of spruce trees here and there overlapped the edge of the Barrens. No Eskimo would stay overnight in the trees for fear of the Indians. Only in daylight would he venture there to pull out the timber he needed for tent poles and other uses, always returning to the Barrens before dusk. This was the custom even into the 1930s. Neither Eskimo nor Cree had any love for the other and wars, sporadic but fierce, had always characterized their relationship. The Crees raided Eskimos and their other northern neighbours, while the Eskimos retaliated on any luckless families or hunting parties whose lesser numbers gave the Eskimos the upper hand. Men were killed outright, and women were either tortured or taken captive as slaves.

96

In the early 1900s, just north of the present post of Eskimo Point, Indian raiding parties surprised some Eskimos on a long point of land near Sentry Island. Cut off from escape, the Eskimos made preparation for defence. Walls of stones were built up, behind which the men could shelter themselves and yet point their arrows at the adversary. The Indians waited until nightfall, when the receding tide allowed them to cross a shallow reach of water, to attack. The outcome was devastating. Only two young Eskimo boys, Eeyak and his friend Ungatok, escaped in kayaks to tell others of their tribe what had befallen their families and relatives. The Eskimos tell also of Indian losses.

Directly opposite the present post of Padley, 150 miles inland, is a high hill, and to this day Eskimos can identify there the bones of Indians who were killed in fierce hand to hand fighting. Sometimes Eskimo children were taken or bought by Indians, who believed that Eskimo girls would grow up to be better sewers than their Indian women. Even in these days of relaxed relations, Eskimo children play a game in which all the players but one draw up in a line, the first in line being the Eskimo mother, the others being her children. The odd one is the "Indian," who has to catch the children one by one, while the mother has to try to prevent him from doing so. The game is based on a legend that describes such an event thought to have taken place. The legend refers to a Chipewyan Indian who was an ogre; but it may have originated, of course, in the years before the Chipewyan actually arrived in the Churchill area, in which case it would refer to the Cree. In any event, the Eskimos regarded both groups as hereditary enemies.

While there was great respect for the Cree as fighters, the Eskimos spoke disparagingly of the Chipewyan. Today most Padlimiut Eskimos know a smattering of the Indian language, but not one of them will demean himself by speaking it.

Small but extraordinary differences existed among Eskimo and Indian customs west of Hudson Bay. For example, Indians whittled wood by drawing the blade toward themselves, using either a short- or a long-handled knife. Eskimos whittled away from themselves, using a straight knife. Eskimo women used their half-moon-shaped knives (ulus) and, holding meat in their teeth, sliced upwards in front of the nose. Indians sliced downwards. It's possible, even likely, that these and other "opposite" differences, though small,

97

Ootootamanga eating, slicing raw caribou meat with her ulu. Eskimo women slice upwards in front of their faces, while Indian women slice downwards. The brass headband is typical of those worn by Padlimiut and Abeamiut women and girls; the brass was likely cut from old primus lamps.

are not accidental, but rather that the Eskimos made sure even in small things that nothing they did could identify them with the Indians. One thing is sure: nowhere — east, west, or in northern Quebec — did the Eskimos look with favour on marriages or any other alliances between the two cultures.

Such an outlook served to maintain a sort of purity in the Eskimo culture, but there were other awesome forces at work that would irrevocably change forever the unique life-style of these northern people.

WHALERS, TRAPPERS, AND TRADERS

Among the early groups who have influenced Eskimo life in the North, none has had such profound impact as the white whalers and traders in search of the North's living commercial resources — whales, white foxes, bears, caribou, walrus, and narwhals. For many years the history of the Canadian North has been the story of the Hudson's Bay Company's attempts to control and exploit this territory and its trade. Independent traders and whalers also came into the eastern Arctic from Scotland, Boston, or San Francisco. Their ships were all too often manned by undesirable and unprincipled men, many of whom had been shanghaied from some waterfront dock and had found themselves on a ship that might not return for a year or more. The captains of these ships were often hard men who ruled their crews every bit as despotically as any dictator.

It was the frequent practice of these captains to call at some place on the Arctic coast and, with promises of high wages, pick up one or two entire Eskimo families to work and hunt throughout the summer and fall whaling season. When it was over, the Eskimo men and older boys spent the winter hunting to keep the whaling crews supplied with fresh meat, while the captain often kept the women as playthings. More often than not, these Eskimo families were later abandoned on some Arctic island with no payment and usually ill-equipped to face life without tools or weapons. Not all whalers were unscrupulous, however; some of them taught the Eskimos how to hunt whales, and some of them sold whaling guns to the Eskimos before they sailed away for other parts. Many a missionary to the Arctic depended on the whaling ships for transportation, often paying for his passage by working as crew.

The impetus for the establishment of the Hudson's Bay Company in the seventeenth century was the European demand for beaver felt hats. However, the era of the trader in the Arctic islands proper and the Barren Lands did not start until much later, when women's fashions called for fur trim and white fox pelts became very valuable. White fox pelts were always more highly priced than coloured fur, because the white ones could be dyed.

The introduction by the whalers and other traders of modern weapons, tools, and matches brought the first white man's goods and thus a change in Eskimo culture. The Eskimos gradually became dependent on these foreign goods, which appeared to provide efficient methods of meeting their needs and which — at least superficially — made their difficult lives somewhat more bearable. Such methods of goods, however, required an ongoing trade relationship with their suppliers if they were to continue to receive the "benefits" of civilization.

It was in the interest of the HBC to take care of the Eskimos who became trappers instead of hunters, providing in the Keewatin District a beautiful annual harvest of white fox pelts. Missions in the North were also recipients of HBC aid in times of difficulty, and transportation to and from the North was always a major help. When I arrived in Eskimo Point in 1926, the HBC trader was firmly entrenched. Much of the old Eskimo life-style remained intact, however, especially the values, beliefs, and ideals.

Trading among the Eskimos naturally began among themselves centuries ago. Every year, until in recent times, groups of many Eskimo tribes would gather in the interior to trade at a place they called Hikolijuak, their traditional meeting place, which lay along a great ridge of land west and inland of the Hudson Bay coastline. Eskimos came from Coppermine with native copper, others from the High North with lamps of soapstone, and some from the northeastern coast with walrus, ivory, and sealskin line. Some traveled south to the Churchill area, which eventually became a major trading centre, particularly with the arrival of the HBC trading post in 1685.

As each summer came and the ice cakes rushed out of the rivers, Eskimo skin boats would make their way down the coast from the north toward Churchill. The unwieldy boats were made with willow for ribs and covered with sealskin. Women rowed them, using long oars made of odd pieces of wood spliced together. Children sat near their mothers while the sled dogs squatted on the household goods and longed to get ashore. Alongside, the men paddled their lean, swift kayaks, ever on the alert for a white whale or the round head of a seal on the grey surface of the sea.

100

Sealskin kayaks of northern Hudson Bay waters. Padlimiut kayaks were made of caribou skin.

People traveled great distances from the north, often arriving late in summer, having come four or five hundred miles from their homes. Their visits to Churchill with furs and skins were sometimes spaced three or even four years apart. Old Arloo told me of long overland treks from the interior near Padley to Churchill in his younger days.

At Churchill for the first time they saw cows at the mission. They saw the great stone walls and the massive stone house inside old Fort Prince of Wales. They handled and threw around the great iron cannon balls that lay in heaps and tried them in the great guns, which had been overturned by the French when they captured the fort without a shot from the British.

Often the Eskimos would feast and the missionary would be invited to join them. When at last all had wiped their hands on a common towel of birdskin, pipes were lit and there was time for him to talk. Stories of the gospel, the singing of hymns, and worship would end the day. And of course, there was trading to be done the following day.

As mentioned, the establishment of trading posts across the Arctic came into being only when white foxes became of value in the market outside. Previously the trading posts had been on the edge of timber, and the Eskimos had spent weeks and even months traveling over the Barren Lands to such outposts as Great Whale River or Churchill. Time wasn't critical to the Eskimos, and on the eastern side of Hudson Bay, for instance, they started from Hudson Strait, wandering southward in October to arrive at the mission station in Moose Factory in March, April, or May for Easter, and then wandering back northward later. During this time, of course, they would hunt and trap and bring in furs to the trading post.

Trading posts were usually established on rivers, by which the trappers could canoe inland and spread over the interior, or from which they moved along the coast; and these trading posts have, in the main, now become centres or settlements. The trading store was a very unpretentious place in earlier days, because it was very difficult to bring in supplies of building materials. Hence, all stores were unheated. Sometimes the stores were painted inside, but most often not. When you entered, you saw kettles and bale handles and even fur hanging from the rafters, while the trade goods would be on the shelves at the back of the counter. The trade goods were displayed but not very attractively, because their appearance really didn't matter.

All supplies were staples, and there were no things in the store that freezing temperature could damage. There were no stoves or other heaters, so everyone dressed in fur clothing. Both trader and purchaser were a bit clumsy because they had to wear mitts all the time. When making entries into his books, however, the trader would often have to shed his

White fox furs piled high at the Hudson's Bay Company post at Eskimo Point, before being baled at "shiptime." Furs were the raison d'être *of the post and the most important item at shiptime.*

mitts; he would make his entry and then blow into his hands to warm them up before putting on the mitts again. The trader also either wore a tuque or pulled up the hood of his parka, just as the Eskimo did who came sometimes with his entire family to trade.

It was the Eskimo father who really did the trading, first for those things that were vitally necessary — tea, cartridges, perhaps a muzzle loader (used as late as the 1930s), some powder and caps for it. Then, having taken care of all the necessities, there would be a certain amount left over to trade, and he might motion to his wife to buy the things she wanted. While such things as weapons and tools were essentials and therefore purchased first, the wife's thoughts would run possibly to a vessel for cooking, but most likely to a tartan shawl which perhaps she'd been looking at for some time. Sometimes she would pick out all the things she wanted — beads, thread, needles, and the goods that were her heart's desire — only to find that she had spent too much and would have to settle in her mind the things she needed most.

The system of payment in the trading post took no account whatsoever of money. Money in the Arctic in early days had no meaning. For the seventeen or eighteen years I lived there, I never once handled even a single dollar bill. I simply charged anything bought in the store, but the trader had a unique system of trading with the Eskimos.

When an Eskimo brought in his foxes, the trader would look them over as well as he could, for often they were just frozen carcasses which the Eskimo had found impossible to thaw and were largely just as they had been taken from the fox traps. Later they would be thawed by the Eskimo post servant, who would strip off the skins, stretch them on shaped boards, dry the pelts and, at the end of the year, bale them for shipment outside. When the trapper brought in the furs, the trader would count them and set out on the counter some article to represent each fox. If a man had twenty foxes, there might be twenty boxes of cartridges set out to symbolize his twenty foxes.

For each fox there would be a number of "skins." A "skin" was worth fifty cents and was represented by a stick about five inches long and half an inch or three-quarters of an inch square. Thus, if a fox pelt was worth twelve dollars, there were twenty-four sticks laid out in a row, and as the Eskimo bought goods, the value of each article was taken from the row of sticks, so that he could always see what he had spent and also what he had left. In this way he wasn't confused, and if later the Eskimo had to return an article, having overbought, the sticks could be replaced accordingly. In some places coins were used, but not official coins of the realm. These coins had marked on them the number of "beaver," as they were called (a beaver was worth fifty cents). Each coin was the equivalent of a stick, but in Eskimo country using sticks was the favoured method because they were less complicated than coins.

If an Eskimo was really affluent, he might purchase a gramophone with records, and many were the hours that the family would spend sitting around listening to records of Harry Lauder, or of reels and jigs. They would play and replay with monotonous regularity the sections on the records where Lauder laughed. These were of great interest, and the Eskimos never seemed to tire of them. The Rev. Edmund Peck made some recordings with the help of the HBC after he had lived in the country some thirty or forty years. At the time he recorded them, he was blind and, quite frankly, had a poor sense of music, but he sang a few hymns and talked to the Eskimos about the "outside" world and the gospel and so maintained contact with the Eskimos. They were great

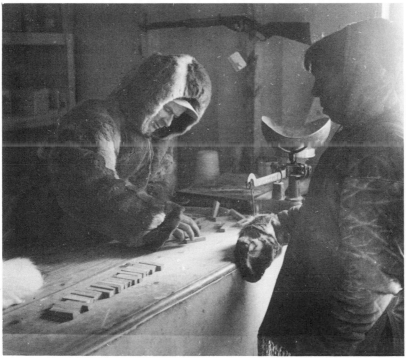

Trading at the HBC post — "skins" set out for barter.

favourites and were replayed at length because they all loved and respected "the good talker."

One of the things I remember about Eskimo Point Store was that no matter how many trade goods were gone by the end of the year, always in the left-hand corner of the ware-house end of the store was a stack of probably twenty-four cases of soap. These were piled to the roof, but every year two more cases of soap would arrive because the district manager considered that if soap hadn't been requisitioned, it must have been forgotten. No Eskimo ever bought soap to wash with, but one or two packages of highly scented soap could be tucked into a box of one's belongings to make it smell nice. The soap wasn't for washing, only for smell.

The Eskimos bought all sorts of things. The Padlimiut and the inland people were reasonably wealthy, because it was nothing for a family to come in with two hundred foxes at the end of the year. Prices paid for a white fox pelt fluctuated according to their demand "outside" but often reached twenty-five or thirty dollars each. An Eskimo's individual take could total a large sum of money indeed, when you consider that they had all the food they wanted from the caribou and had no concern at all about such things as home mortgages and fuel bills. Trapping for foxes thus gave them a tremendous lot of pin money such as no white person in the north country could ever expect to earn. But the concept of saving for a rainy day was never a part of Eskimo thinking. If they had the money to trade, they would use it.

Not all the Eskimos trapped; there were one or two exceptions. There was an Eskimo traveling salesman who came from far inland at Ennadai Lake, for example. Having trapped foxes only in the fall, he would take them into the trading post and with the money buy various supplies that were small or light in weight and so could be easily transported — such goods as tea, cartridges, cloth goods, and so on. He would then make his way across the land to the bay coast. On the way he would trade at exorbitant prices the goods he had bought in the store. A pound of tea, for instance, might be worth one fox — as much as thirty dollars. If no one wanted to buy, he would simply move on to the next camp and so, with a number of stops, finally arrive at at the coast, where he would trade more goods for the pelts he'd acquired. After a few days he'd start wandering back to sell his newly obtained wares. At the end of winter he had quite a profit, which enabled him to last through spring and summer in greater affluence than any of his neighbours.

Another Eskimo trader at Perry River became quite famous for his habit of ordering cases of goods by taking the name that was on the case and ordering it from "outside." He posed problems to the suppliers with such orders as "24 tins 1-½ s." He achieved considerable fame in this way, because he did quite well as a trader. One day, however, he became drunk and killed his best friend. He had no idea he'd done it but afterward was willing to agree that he must have. Thus ended his trading career.

For the rest of the Eskimos, trade in fox furs provided virtually the only means of obtaining southern goods. The western side of Hudson Bay was an excellent place to trap the white foxes, because they followed the caribou herds and scavenged off the dead animals — but they also hung around the caches the Eskimos made. In fall and spring the foxes would often migrate, and in such migrations the Eskimos could amass a tremendous number of foxes in a very short time. I remember one man telling me he had caught 125 foxes in less than a week and that they had to drive foxes away with whips from the carcasses of walrus that they had summer-cached on the shore, while they removed foxes from the traps, because the free foxes were fighting and spoiling the fur of those who were caught. At times it's possible to see fox tracks everywhere down the coast, as they migrate from one place to another just before denning up in the spring. There is a fluctuation in the number of foxes about every fourth year, which tends to be a peak for numbers caught. The following year is usually almost a failure, and for the next two years the numbers gradually build up again. This cycle apparently applies all over the Arctic.

There were times when the Eskimos had very little food and faced temporary hunger and hardship. There would be certain things in their possession that were of value and could be sold to others who wished to buy them. Sinew, shoes, skins, and various objects made by the Eskimo would be sold in the store, and the trader would allow the owner an amount in trade for the value of these objects. The store, however, never made a profit when these items were sold back to an Eskimo who needed them, and thus the trader served the community when there was need and helped in situations that could have been quite hard on the Eskimo people. The traders, in common with the missionaries, encouraged the Eskimos to get off onto the land or away from the post to hunt and trap, to be self-reliant, to maintain their own way of life and to retain it. The Eskimos did this, and because they were able to live as Eskimos, it was possible for them to keep their independence, which some peoples in the world have found difficult to do.

WARM PEOPLE, COLD LAND

Perhaps nowhere else in the world is there a group of people who have learned so much about how to survive in such a harsh land with so little material help — in spite of the trading posts. Life in the Arctic depends on careful decisions and an intimate understanding of the world that envelops its inhabitants, because their environment tolerates few mistakes. But like people everywhere, they occasionally do make mistakes. And even small errors can be grave enough for the perpetrator to pass out of the picture. In the basic areas of food, clothing, shelter, and transportation, mistakes or miscalculations could mean death. With this knowledge firmly in mind, the Eskimo endures in the Arctic.

Travel in the North, for both Eskimos and particularly the white "newcomers," has always been difficult and dangerous. Errors could and did come in travel, because many are the miles between settlements and over the great, limitless spaces that one travels. Those spaces are impressive, for it may well be forty, fifty, or even two hundred miles before one sees another human being or reaches another dwelling. The isolation that tends to overwhelm a person in these spaces throws you back on the comradeship and friendliness of your fellow traveler and a deep closeness develops, whether he is Eskimo or white.

Generally a white person becomes very dependent on an Eskimo traveling companion, largely because of the former's alarming lack of expertise in the subtleties of Arctic survival. The seemingly endless winter sled journeys are broken by overnight stops in igloos built under the magic of your companion's knife, and you're especially grateful for his skill.

It's true that any man who has never cared enough to learn the language of his Eskimo companion may find it a lonely time, but when the average missionary travels, it's almost always with an Eskimo, one of his "flock." He journeys with someone whom he feels he can rely on, as I did with Sam, and whom he can speak with, not only of everyday things but also of deeper things of the spirit. When under the warm rays of a spring sun one sits in security and companionable silence with his Eskimo traveling companion, contemplation is pleasant. For he learns with the Eskimos that there's no need always to be talking, something which those living in the Arctic realize is a great part of life in the South.

Little questions, however, often come to mind regarding the life of the people of each other's race. There was the day on the trail, for instance, when my Eskimo friend Sam quietly broke a silence intruded upon only by the hiss of sled runners as they glided over the snow. He exclaimed, "That woman in the Churchill Post Office has fingernails like blood. Do they grow like that, or did she make them that way?" I assured him they were painted, but I was unprepared for the "Why?" that followed. It was difficult to explain until I remembered the tribal facial tattoo markings of old Eskimo women and asked him why Eskimos of early days suffered the pain on their faces of a needle threaded with caribou sinew dipped in soot. The reply, "To make them beautiful," enabled me to explain that the same was true of white women. The grunt of derisive acknowledgement indicated his acceptance of the reason but his rejection of the idea.

We were a little farther on our way, both of us seated on the sled and the dogs contentedly trotting along in the traces of the hitch. The dogs had an advance of thirty feet or so. Heat from the sun made us drowsy, despite twenty below temperatures. Before I knew it I was lying on my back, my legs propped up by the overturned sled and my feet hanging over my head. Very close to my feet I could see Sam's feet also waving in the air. Suddenly he began to laugh. "Lots and lots of feet," he joked and went into paroxysms of laughter. He remembered the incident for years afterwards. Many, many are the little ordinary things that tell of the ready, delightful humour of the Eskimos, both on and off the trail.

There's no better man than an Eskimo to be on hand in a time of trial and difficulty. His past experience always gives him a background on which to draw in any difficult situation. If, for example, you take your mitts off when lashing something onto a sled, the mitts freeze almost immediately, and at once your hands are severely cold, especially when the temperature is well below zero. Without a word your traveling companion draws off his warm gloves, tosses them to you, catches your frozen ones, puts them on his own warm hands to thaw them, and when they're warm, tosses them back with a smile. In the Arctic, you learn to be generous.

The Eskimo's warm generosity includes awarding his white guest, who usually sleeps outstretched in bed, the central and therefore the warmest place on the sleeping bench. Should the white man's legs be too long even in the central place, then it's quite likely the host will open the side of the igloo and build a special little extension for the feet.

When traveling, the Eskimo is most considerate of the warmth of his traveling companion. If it's a white man, he'll constantly check to find out whether or not the other is cold, simply because he himself is cold at the beginning of a journey. It's interesting that when a white man starts out from his house the first day on the trail, he's warm because his reserves of heat energy are high. The Eskimo, however, has been living in an unheated igloo and feels the cold but gradually gets used to it, so by the second or third day he begins to feel warmer. By that time the white man, with his resistance lowered, feels very cold and becomes colder yet. This continues until — and if ever — the white man also becomes habituated to the northern climate.

Two men on the same sled seldom sit on it together if there is anything approaching a heavy load. They take turns riding and jogging alongside; when one is tired of jogging, he drops onto the sled. His companion then jumps off and runs alongside. This trading off becomes almost instinctive on the trail, because one naturally puts into practice that great principle that all sensible travelers soon learn in the Arctic: it's necessary to share.

The stopover for the night is also a shared operation, and when at last the light's out, the silence of the night is broken only by crunching snow as a dog rises to shake his back or curl up more comfortably. It's then that one feels a great sense of comradeship. In spite of hundreds of nights spent in igloos, often a hundred or more miles from the nearest habitation, I've never had a sense of loneliness on the trail, but rather the realization that there was a warmhearted relationship between myself and my guide. I've seldom felt it elsewhere, this comradeship equaled only by boundless hospitality. This hospitality is endless in Eskimo homes.

In my experience, a host always offered the best he had, no matter how short of food the family might be. One day I entered an igloo far in the interior, and I was bidden welcome with a firm handshake. I noticed that the family looked rather thin. The mug of tea they offered me was so pale that it appeared they had reboiled some used tea leaves from the shelf where they were stored frozen, for emergencies. Quietly my host said he was sorry they had no fresh meat such as the white man liked, for hunting had been bad in the fall. His wife brought in a caribou skin, well worn with age. She placed on it a pile of caribou rib bones. The dried meat was covered with mould, which showed they were living on last summer's caches.

Life on the Barrens was often generally similar to this situation, though the specifics differed. There was the lady who asked me if I liked marrow from bones of caribou legs. I replied that yes, I loved it, and she suggested I move from the snow bench on which I was sitting and lift the skin that covered it and I would find some marrow there. I did so and found a skin bag by no means clean, in which were dozens of little cylinders resembling broken sticks of dynamite. They averaged about two inches long, all very black and grubby. This was marrow taken from leg bones boiled some six months before. Immediately my desire for marrow vanished. So did my vision of a nice marrow bone filled with rich, fresh marrow fat. But it was the best delicacy she had to offer, and I was welcome to it. I ate some and thanked her for her gift.

Not only are Eskimos hospitable to an extreme; they tell the truth. If an Eskimo tells the truth in an embarrassing or troubling situation, seldom will a white man believe his native friend has been naive enough to speak it. Blatant truth obviously could get a white man into trouble, and he might want to avoid that. To the Eskimo, however, the truth is the truth, and if he's asked a question he must answer it truthfully. The white man doesn't think it possible for a man to be so foolish, so he probably won't believe the Eskimo.

The Inuktitut language isn't as illogical as ours, and so often the Eskimo is taken to be giving an untruthful answer, when frequently it's because he's been asked in our peculiar way a negative question. "Did you not do this?" or "Didn't you do this?" (which is the same question) might be asked. The Eskimo answers, "No," meaning that he did. To him two negatives make a positive, but the white man usually takes it to mean that he's replied negatively. (If you're unsure of what I mean, just ask yourself the question, "Didn't you have breakfast?" or "Did you have breakfast?" Whether or not you did, the answer to both questions will likely be the same.) There's much misunderstanding and confusion in the use of negatives, particularly double negatives.

To write in general terms about any ethnic group may be considered by some to be too simplistic to represent real people, for well we know that groups are made up of individuals and each one, while at the same time part of the group, is different, unique. To generalize is possible, however, for there are some physical and cultural characteristics common to all in any such group. This is true of our Eskimo friends. They have developed ways of doing certain things which are effective in their lives and which preserve their culture, community, family, and self.

For example, Eskimos have a body language of their own, adapted for their own situations. If a hunter has spied caribou from the top of a rise and companions are too far away for talking or yelling, he raises two arms above his head to resemble caribou horns, as a sign. Standing sideways, a man moving his arms up and down in front of himself makes a sign to his friends to come ahead and advance to him. Waving his arms above his head up and down to shoulder height is a sign to remain still. This is particularly used as a warning of danger.

Perhaps the most commonly used sign of all is that of approval, when one raises the eyebrows almost imperceptibly and makes the eyes seem rounder than usual. This is a favourite gesture of children when they give assent to a question. They seldom speak if they can do this. On the other hand, if they want to say "No," they just blink their eyes, which is something white people seldom understand, and they think that the child is perhaps being sullen when it refuses to speak.

One of the ideas that the Eskimo holds in contrast with ours is judgement of distance. We measure things in standard inches, feet, yards, or miles. To the Eskimo, distance is relative and compared with the distance he has just come. So if he's traveled twenty miles and there are still ten miles to go, it's not very far. But if he's inside a settlement and it's a question of meeting someone at the other end, perhaps a quarter-mile away, then it's a long way to go. Long distances are reckoned by sleeps, meaning the number of times a person sleeps at night traveling between one place and another. Roughly, one can reckon twenty or thirty miles a day of travel by dog team as one "sleep."

Arngnarowyuk once spent a whole day in our kitchen watching my wife, accepting many mugs of tea, biscuits, and her efforts to speak Inuktitut. Finally he prepared to leave, hurriedly got up, slammed the door and was gone. A minute or two later he was back. He gingerly reopened the door a crack and asked, "Tell me, how far did you go to get your wife?" How could he comprehend the distance from London, England, by ship, train, and a schooner to Eskimo Point? Only by the number of sleeps. Satisfied but by no means convinced, his passing comment of incredulity was, "Couldn't you get one any closer?"

The most remarkable thing of all is that when an Eskimo travels, he's able to tell exactly the time he'll arrive in camp or at your home. This exactness is extraordinary in that there are dozens of things that could throw off his calculations. He has to consider the speed of his dogs and their condition, the type of land over which they must travel, the nature and direction of winds, the condition of the snow, temperatures, the weight of his load, whether or not the sled runners will be pulling well, and the like. Even with these constraints and in spite of being almost twenty miles away, the Eskimo can tell you his time of arrival almost to the minute.

An Eskimo's sight is usually extraordinary as well. When an Eskimo says there's a sled approaching, the average white man can't see it. When the sled is near enough for you to see, he can tell you how many dogs are pulling it. When you can see the tiny black dots of the dogs, by that time he can tell you the identity of the man driving it. This keen-sightedness serves the Eskimo well, particularly when he's out hunting.

Some Eskimos claim to be able to see things at incredible distances. Just after the turn of the century, an old man appeared at the door of the Royal Northwest Mounted Police inspector's house at Fort Churchill. The man announced that three white men were at Broad River. One of them, he claimed, swam across the river and paddled back in a cached canoe so that the other two might cross. Then he added, "They will be here in Churchill in ten days' time." The inspector laughed, because Broad River was miles to the south. The idea itself was preposterous; the only ship of the year had long since gone; one would have to go nearly a thousand miles south to see more white men; and lastly, it was now fall and near freeze-up. The old Eskimo was used to the white man's not believing him, but to prove his point he reiterated his story. Moreover, he gave descriptions of all three men, the colour of their hair and details of their clothing. The inspector was impressed enough to enter the incident in his diary but remained unconvinced.

Ten days later three white men arrived in Churchill. They fitted the old Eskimo's descriptions precisely. Yes, they had been at Broad River ten days ago, and one had swum the river to get the canoe cached on the other side. They were surveyors who had been caught within the country late in the season; they had made their way to Churchill because it was the nearest post they knew of and the only place for shelter for the winter. But how did the old Eskimo know? He simply said, "I saw them." But how? His explanation suggested that he saw things in his mind but not with his eyes. Such clairvoyance appears to be fairly common among older Eskimos.

At Maguse River lived a dear old Eskimo woman who was completely blind. Though she had a stick with which she could feel her way, she had to be helped around by other people to avoid the boulders and stones strewn on the landscape. As a result, she spent hours just sitting in contemplation, as do blind people everywhere. One day, as she was sitting quietly in her tent, she began to tell the others present that she could see Peters, the HBC store manager from Padley post, trying to cross an ice-bound lake (she named it) in a canoe. She went on to describe the portage he was making with his canoe, because a welter of upturned ice blocked the way along the shores of the lake. He and his two Eskimo helpers were carrying bundles of fur across a neck of land to where a boat had been left in the fall. She told of their shock when they found the motorboat, their hope for transportation, damaged by the ice. The boat was a useless wreck.

She described how they then began packing the canoe with furs and food for the long journey to the coast. She was able to tell her listeners the names of the men accompanying the post manager. This was in the days before radio was used, and no normal communication was possible. Her story soon was relayed to the manager in the local store, who'd been worried for days about the late arrival of these men from the interior. He considered it nonsense, of course; he was convinced that Peters would arrive from the interior in the morning. But the old lady declared that the fur brigade wouldn't arrive for eight days.

Day after day passed, but there was no sign of the boat. On the eighth day, just as the old woman had foretold, Peters arrived — by canoe, rather than boat — with the two helpers whom the old woman had said would be with him. They had found their boat damaged and useless. They gave the details of their trek across the point and the time it took them; all details were correct to the last degree. Peters and the local store manager were two very astonished men after they compared their notes. How did the old lady know? Second sight? Could she actually see at a great distance things that were

114

happening? But she was blind. And even if this is the answer, what's always puzzled me is how both she and the old man of the previous story knew in advance exactly how many days it would take for the travelers to arrive. It's rough country; delays often happen; and yet the forecasts were extraordinarily precise. There are many things about the lives of the old Eskimos which we white people will likely never understand. Yet, both stories were found to be truthful, and this is consistent with Eskimo standards. That we should be able to understand.

Besides being truthful, the Eskimo tends to be quite conservative, measuring his acceptance of events by things that have happened in the past. This is exemplified in an occurrence that took place in the early days of my arrival at Eskimo Point, when an Eskimo came and asked me what I thought about drum dancing. Was it all right for the Eskimos to have a drum dance or not? Not knowing too much about it, I replied that I thought drum dancing was quite all right and good to do, provided it wasn't bound up in the worship of evil spirits, which was the case in old times. The Eskimo who had asked me turned and said, "You are just like the missionary from Churchill. Years ago he said that too, and so you are the right missionary." Such was his confirmation of my opinion; and the validity — which he accepted — was gauged by the consistency of the response.

Eskimos hold all things as common property. You may borrow from an Eskimo anything he owns, provided he's not using it. It's this sort of idea the white men like, that we can use everything belonging to the Eskimos. Many of us act accordingly and borrow at will, but we don't accept, on the other hand, that anything of the white man's that the Eskimo wants can be his. If you want to take his cache of meat because you're hungry or have to feed your dogs, it's quite all right with the Eskimo who owns it, as long as you tell him. If you take it and fail to say anything about it when you next meet him, however, then you've stolen.

One of the outstanding traits of an Eskimo is his pure politeness. He'll never upset you if he can help it; this wouldn't be polite. Therefore, he'll try to make you feel that he'll do what you request. Sometimes he'll simply ignore a request that he believes to be unreasonable, thereby eliminating the need to upset the person asking the favour by refusing. You can't drive an Eskimo to do anything. You can work with him, but you can't make him do your will; equality, after all, is working together. Eskimos have always had a confidence in themselves, a trait built by the needs of men to feel that they can conquer and maintain dominion in a grim and hard country. An Eskimo is a man, an inuk of the Inuit.

CHAPTER FIVE

THE LIFE
THAT WAS

THE FAMILY FOUNDATION

The family unit in Eskimo life is critically important. It's the very foundation, the structural backbone of the people. To fully appreciate this, one must realize that the Eskimos live in the hardest, most difficult land in the world and have survived. By a process of what some might call natural selection they have materially and mentally survived as only the best of the race, for the weaklings in body and spirit died. If a man wasn't fitted for the grim life of fighting for a living, sooner or later and in one way or another, nature would overwhelm him. For most of the year individual families separated themselves from other members of their loose communities; their food resources were widely scattered and a dispersed hunting pattern was most effective for surviving the long winters. If a man couldn't stand the rigours of hours, days, and weeks spent alone or with his family, he failed and nature disposed of him — and, often, his dependants. The strength of the society rested on the family, and each member had roles to perform for its maintenance. The family is the future of the race; the children will one day be the future — and security for the aged — but only the strong will survive with the heritage of the father passed on to the son, and that of the mother to the daughter.

But life has always been difficult for the Eskimos, even at the moment of birth for a Padlimiut infant, when the risk was great in the old days. Damage to an unborn child was frighteningly frequent, for the Padlimiut used rather cruel and dangerous practices at childbirth. At the first signs of labour, usually before the end of full term, a rope was placed around the pregnant woman just below the breasts and knotted tightly. Then, with her kneeling with legs apart, her upstretched arms held by two women (often female anga-koks), the rope was forced downwards until the child was expelled. All too often the infant's rib cage was crushed in this process, or the woman would be so badly injured that she might hemorrhage and die. Even if she lived, the newborn child would usually be premature and often too weak and injured to survive.

Winifred had had training in midwifery in England before coming to Eskimo Point, but the Eskimos rarely called her to assist at births, and then only when the angakoks and native midwives had failed. I recall an occasion during the latter years of our ministry there in which she was asked to help at a birth. Caroline, an Aivilingmiut girl married to an Eskimo special constable in the RCMP (both she and her husband were Christians), was fearful of the local Padlimiut birthing practice and wanted nothing to do with it. Caroline's time came, and she sent someone to ask for Winifred's help. As Win ploughed through the deep, melting snow to the tent, she saw a scene reminiscent of Christ on the Mount of Olives. On the surrounding bare ground near the tent were men, women, and children sitting around muttering and murmuring as she passed. The flap sides of the tent were rolled up all around, exposing the interior. Inside were Caroline and her mother-in-law (also a Christian Aivilingmiut), all the camp midwives and angakoks. Win stopped, looked around, and asked Caroline, "Do you want to have your baby this way?" The answer was a quick "No!" Win politely asked the angakoks and midwives to leave and then rolled down the tent flaps, restoring privacy. Quickly and smoothly (and without ropes) the newborn baby appeared, a beautiful boy of 7½ pounds. Caroline's mother-in-law carried out the entire procedure.

This experience marked a real breakthrough in birth practices among the Padlimiut. The younger pregnant women looked with envy — and anticipation for themselves — on the size and strength of Caroline's baby, which she proudly carried in her parka pouch. At birth he was equivalent in size to the average three-month-old Padlimiut baby. In subsequent years Caroline and her husband gave birth to six strong sons, six potential hunters. Slowly, by teaching and encouragement, the cruel ways of the past began to change for the good of the people.

If the birth were successful by whatever method, the baby would be nursed at the mother's breast, securely cra-

Caroline Gibbons with her healthy first-born son, Jimmy, born naturally at full term, without the use of ropes. Caroline subsequently bore five more sons, all beautiful children and potential hunters.

dled in her lap and warm within the folds of the voluminous, tent-like parka, under which she could attend to all his needs. When sleep time came, the parka was slung back to front, the baby arranged in the pouch, tiny legs crossed on a thick pad of caribou skin which acted as a diaper. By mother's simply easing the garment around, the baby could lie naked on her warm, bare back. A skin thong with a large wooden, ivory, or horn toggle on each end was looped outside the parka under the sitting child and fastened to two loops of skin line attached at the shoulders and reaching to the breasts. This held and supported the child. No baby kangaroo could be more secure.

In common with mothers the world over, the Eskimo woman crooned and rocked her baby to sleep, with the baby either in the pouch or held in her arms. Mother might sing a little lullaby while pacing back and forth, often with a side-stepping jig, adding a little pat on the baby's bottom. Soon baby would be asleep. Eskimo songs, which include lullabies, usually have words sung in a rather monotonous outburst followed by rhythmic repetitions of "Yah, yah! yah ee yah!" This form of singing is also used in the songs of the drum dance.

There has always been a very close association between mother and baby in the culture of the Eskimos. The child is carried in the pouch of her inner coat, which will be its home for several years. This pouch (amaot) on a woman's back is seldom empty. A few women conceive every year. But a new-born child can't be looked after if the pouch is already occupied by a one-year-old. Temperatures outside the pouch, mind you, are usually well below the freezing mark, even inside the Eskimo's home. There are two alternatives for the newcomer: adoption or death. Someone would always be anxious to adopt a boy, a potential hunter and provider for later in life. But in times past, a girl baby was often placed in a snowdrift to die, not because the mother didn't want the child, but because she was unable to care for it. If the child were adopted, it had to be by a woman able to suckle it or prepared to wean an older child. The new baby would be brought up by the foster mother as her own, but sometimes she herself would give birth to another child and her own newborn baby would then have to be adopted by someone else, because the adopted child already occupied the amaot in her hood. The matter of biological parentage could become extremely confusing. In general, adopted children were raised into the family and both cherished and cared for.

In keeping with their belief that all children are young adults, mothers, when smoking, pass the pipe back over their shoulders holding the stem so that the child can take a puff. A baby of eighteen months might do this, though it wouldn't be a very vigorous puff. As a young child grows, clothing progresses from just a hat to a little jacket for play around in the igloo and finally to a one-piece garment or coverall. Until puberty children are considered sexless, and all taboos and other prohibitions that apply to their parents don't affect them at all, as there are no taboos on youngsters; but there are taboos that the mother must observe at the time of birth and for various periods as a child grows up, particularly when a child becomes ill.

Like children in the South, a young child may become very precocious and want to show off. This of course is plainly obvious to the adults, who immediately frown at the child and become very busy talking about other things and completely ignore him. After a little while the child will usually grow very quiet and then, with a rather hang-dog expression, go across to mother or father, indicating that the tantrum is finished. The child is then usually drawn close, given a kiss by rubbing noses, and perhaps provided with a particularly nice tidbit, such as the eye of a caribou or a piece of tongue. With this gesture the parents dismiss the child's misbehaviour, and the little one is now reinstated in their good graces. Thus the parents show approval of good behaviour and also consistent discipline. Ostracism, or temporary shunning of the child, is so effective that children seldom if ever need to be spanked; this is true even of adopted children, who become part of the family unit. Rarely does an adopted child take a lesser place in the family than natural children of the parents.

Children hear everything in family life and in community life; a large igloo might hold three or four families without partitions, so that everything done and said, including all kinds of squabbles, is quite openly seen and shared by everyone. Matrimonial tiffs are considered an affair of the couple themselves, but because everyone knows of them, they are commented on in general. Since the earliest times there has been no secrecy about anything in life, either in matters of sex, marital behaviour, raising children, or anything else. The children at an early age learn the anatomy of animals, for they watch their parents skin and dissect animals. As soon as boys or girls become old enough they are taught how to do this themselves and so they watch, comment, and learn. They must learn how to skin seals, caribou, polar bears, and foxes, some of which will be traded at the HBC store. Very early in life girls learn how to use the ulu, while boys become expert with an ordinary knife.

Mothers lavish love and care upon their children, often

121

From an early age, children must learn the skills they will need to survive in the Arctic. Winifred was fascinated by the dexterous young hands that removed the skin from a weasel, and sketched a boy absorbed in the task.

giving them soft clothing beautifully made and decorated with beads or coloured patterns of fur. Mothers spend hours working the skins to make them just as soft and warm as possible. It's natural, of course, that a good hunter has better clothes for his children than a poorer hunter, but the children always get the best.

There was a trapper who came to Eskimo Point over the land who discovered an igloo with no dogs outside, although there was a sled and dog harness. The igloo was holed up securely tight, and blizzards had nearly covered it with snow. The absence of dogs but the presence of a sled suggested that the family might be dead, for no one came out when he drew up alongside with his team. When the visitor opened up the igloo he found a father, mother, and two small children with absolutely nothing to eat; they had given up all hope of survival. Their dogs were long since dead and they had no food whatsoever. They were so hungry that even though they shared food from the traveler, the children fastened onto the fish bones that were thrown away and chewed them up too; but the children were in far better shape than their parents, for they had been given as much as possible for as long as the food lasted.

I remember going to Baker Lake one day and looking out the window of the mission at a man who stood with a skin bedroll and a rifle slung across his back, holding onto a leash with a dog. As I looked out, the dog flopped down in exhaustion and the man stood there and then reached behind him and hauled up the snowbank a little boy about seven years old. Behind the boy stood an old woman. I called to the old man, telling him to come in, but all he could say was, "I'm cold, I'm cold." At last they came into the mission kitchen. The old man tottered in and sat down. The woman, too, looked very weak. The young boy didn't appear to be in terribly poor shape, and I wondered whether the old man was sick. When I asked him, he said, "No, I'm just hungry." For four days they had walked, a distance of at least eighty miles, and neither of them except the child had had anything to eat, and he had had very little indeed. We had to keep him forcibly from eating very much, because otherwise it might have killed him. When I remarked about how well the little boy looked compared to the old man who had been starving, the man indignantly said, "Of course we feed our children first, and while there's food, we give to them." How true this appeared to be, for the little boy had rosy cheeks and looked as though he hadn't suffered at all. This sacrifice is typical of the Eskimos' love and care for their children. If only parents in other lands would care as much.

THE IMPERATIVE OF MARRIAGE

When a young girl reached the time of puberty, she began to wear a parka just like her mother's, but with no amaot for a baby. The lower end of the tail, which almost swept the ground, would be cut square to the bottom, turned inward and suspended by two ropes of sinew or wool from just below the shoulder blades. This kind of parka indicated she was now of marriageable age but not yet married. No one could even consider her as a future bride except the young man, perhaps years her senior or even her junior, to whom she had been promised at birth. Parents arranged marriages for their children, because women were in short supply and a man needed to be certain of having a bride. The marriage promises were ostensibly binding and strictly adhered to —

and annulled only by the death of either party or outright incompatibility between the partners. Because communities were small, everyone knew that the two would marry. It was the accepted procedure and considered normal in young people's lives.

To the Eskimos marriage was simply a practical relationship between a man and a woman and it began without a wedding ceremony. At marriage a girl simply moved her belongings into the dwelling of her new husband's parents, with whom they lived for the first few years. Often the newlyweds would be quite young, no more than twelve or thirteen years old. But they lived together as man and wife, and each knew what had to be done to survive. The Eskimo wife at this early age fetched water, gathered moss, and learned to do all the sewing for her husband, besides the cooking and preparation of skins for clothing and general chores for her husband's parents. During this apprenticeship, young and beautiful girls often aged very quickly.

Marriage for the Eskimos was always a state in which the couple must live amicably together or part company. This was a perfectly understandable view. The family might be isolated, far from neighbours, and the married couple might be the only two adults in a large area. If they weren't compatible, something explosive would be bound to happen, for isolated people must be happy spiritually as well as mentally. Therefore, if a couple didn't get along well, they would part company after a trial run, and the wife could return to her parents' home. Seldom did this happen if a child was born to the union, however, for the love of children created a bond between parents.

There were cases where women and men seemed indeed incompatible, and an older Eskimo told me of one of these in a sage observation: "So-and-so couldn't get on well with his first wife. This was fine, but today he left his third wife, and it must be his fault. From now on no one will give his daughter to him in marriage because he must be bad to live with. If he hasn't been able to get on with three, he won't get on with anyone else." His only chance to find a wife would be to go to a distant place and find an old woman or widow with no chance for a local partner.

When a couple split up the children, if any, might be adopted or cared for by the parents of the girl, who would resume her life as one of the family in her old home. After some time, perhaps, a man in another tribe might hear of her single status and travel or send word that he would like her for a wife. She might then be taken to live far away, but not before she had shown her modesty by trying to run away or hide after she had been placed on the sled by her father.

One of the men from the Shownukromiut tribe had two wives, which is fairly common among Eskimo men. I asked him how he'd come to have two wives rather than one. He explained that he took one woman for his wife, and traveling along the coast they came across his wife's sister, who'd been abandoned by her husband, which also is fairly common. This Shownukromiut man therefore accepted her as his second wife, and she bore him five children; incidentally, his first wife was barren. Both wives lived amicably with each other (an uncommon state of affairs in such cirumstances), perhaps because they were sisters.

While polygyny (two or more wives) was a common form of polygamy in the Arctic, polyandry, or a wife's having more than one husband, wasn't unknown. This situation was caused usually by necessity. Perhaps a man had no one to sew his clothing or to repair it, no one to look after food preparation, and no home to return to, all of which, quite apart from sexual aspects, put pressure on a man to find a wife. Some men would search for years from one tribe to another but not find a wife. For polyandry to work, two men had to care about each other enough to share a wife — and one can imagine her being very wise in sharing favours evenly — but such situations did exist for many Eskimo men in the Arctic. A woman with two husbands would be provided with many material things in life, and she would become well off with two men to provide skins for clothing, utensils, tools, and, above all, food. Children born of such unions suffered no discrimination; they were like all other children, accepted as such and cared for and devotedly looked after.

Sometimes, but not often, a child might be treated as a drudge and forced to get water and do the chores, but in the main these were women's tasks, though often the children enjoyed helping. Children were cherished not only for themselves but because when they grew up they would look after the old people who could no longer hunt, and so a son was welcomed and often spoiled beyond measure.

Eskimos show little or no affection in public, even when

a man leaves his wife to set off on the trail, no matter how long he'll be gone. He might make some remark or not, and the same is true when he comes back from a long trip. Only once, when I went to enter the church, I surprised in the porch a young couple who had been married for several years. They drew back from each other with scarlet faces, for one simply did not show affection in front of someone else. Children and the elderly escape this prohibition, however. Old people may display love and affection to a person they may not have seen for a long time, holding them tightly in a hugging embrace. Such expressions of love are usually demonstrated only in exceptional circumstances or in a family situation.

In the early days an Eskimo would beat his wife for marital infidelity. If he lent her to a friend, however, there would be no immorality. Indeed, he would most likely reply to any concern by saying, "She's no different now from what she was, so why talk about it?"

In Eskimo life there's great sharing between men and women. They help each other in the tasks of raising a family and in everyday life. Scraping skins, for example, is a difficult task and one that requires strength. It's traditionally the woman's task, but a husband usually won't hesitate to take over and scrape at the skins, often till the sweat pours off his brow and he's very tired. The skins have to be scraped to make them soft and pliable for clothing, and a man benefits from his own work, of course, because a soft garment is warm, and this applies to his own as well as his wife's clothing. A man might set out or arrive home from the trail, but it will be his wife who helps harness or hitch the dogs, not because it's part of her job but because she wants to help. The men will cut up the meat, although traditionally this is part of woman's work. In a thousand and one ways they help each other if the occasion calls for it and there is need.

A WOMEN'S FEAST

When a community consists of several families, the men and women feast separately; first men, then women and children. The children don't always choose to eat with their parents, especially in larger communities. But single families eat together, off by themselves. Visitors are invited to join in. Meal times aren't at any prearranged hour; Eskimos snack when they're hungry. The mother isn't always sure a child

Heeotoroot harnesses a dog, preparatory to her husband's setting out on a sled trip. This is one of the jobs women consider to be particularly theirs and is one of the many ways that they help their husbands.

will be there, although she knows the little one is never far away. I've been in Eskimo homes during winter and been invited to eat with them thirteen or fourteen times a day. But even in times of plenty, cooked meat is never served more than once a day, if at all.

One day while I was visiting in Aoalogoot's home, the igloo door swung open. A young girl with rosy cheeks excitedly announced, "Come, come, there's a feast at Mary's." Aoalogoot had anticipated the invitation and so hadn't eaten. Now she hurriedly pulled on her shoes, adjusted her attigi and belt, sticking bare arms into the sleeves, and slithered along the long snow passageway, bent almost double to avoid scraping rime from the roof. The passage led to the always open front of the outer porch and into the brilliant glare of daylight.

Some two hundred feet away was Mary's igloo. Smoke rose from the three-foot chimney of snow, blackened near the top and through cracks between the snow blocks.

Pimyuk squeezes through the tiny entrance to Aoalogoot's igloo to invite her to the feast at Mary's igloo.

Through the base I could see the red flames of the fire burning inside.

A procession of women and girls scrambled down the tunnel into the igloo, laughing and coughing as they passed the small cooking igloo, its acrid smoke billowing from inside. It was Mary's pleasure to provide a women's feast, and she invited all to enter. Usually, men did not participate in women's feasts, but I was invited as a special guest. Soon everyone was present, murmuring approval when they saw the cooking pot, half of a ten-gallon drum. It was filled with caribou heads (with much skin still on) and the ribs, legs, and shoulders of a caribou, all nicely cooked. Many bones stuck out of the top, which was covered with a fine layer of white ash from the burning willow twigs used as fuel.

A great, carved wooden tray crafted years ago from spliced tree trunks was piled with meat and put in the centre of the sleeping bench. The women settled comfortably around it. Each reached into her hood and found her ulu. At the invitation of the lady of the house, "Pray you, eat," everyone fell to.

Pieces that caught the eye of guests were soon taken. A woman would place a piece of meat between her teeth and sever it by drawing the ulu upward just in front of her lips. (A southerner, I'm sure, would slice off the tip of the nose eating this way.) There wasn't much talking for quite a while, until the hostess produced mugs and passed around broth or soup in which the caribou had been boiled. Gossip time came when the tea kettle arrived. The kettle was aluminum but hardly recognizable as such, being black and covered with encrustations of soot. The outside indicated the colour of the contents: the tea, generously added to the kettle by the handful, was always boiled for a full twenty minutes. A ten-pound sack of sugar quickly diminished, because most guests preferred four or five teaspoonfuls per mug. Then Mary brought out a few delicacies — a little dried meat and some fat stored in the intestines of a caribou (which is really tasty) — and placed them on the bench. Finally each woman produced her pipe and lit it. There was time now for talk.

Naturally, children hear all the gossip, and they learn from among all the things discussed by the adults. With the lack of privacy in Eskimo culture, their children might have a far healthier understanding of life than those of southerners.

At last Mary's feast was over. The children ran off to play, and the good neighbours drifted away home. A feast for men is much the same, except that women of the household wait on the men. Only when the feast is over do the children eat, because these are times of plenty and there is enough for everyone.

SHARING THE LOAD

When the women met for their feasts and their frequent teas, they talked in a special "language" supposedly known to them alone and which men wouldn't demean themselves to speak. Many discussions were of community affairs, and these deliberations were very influential, if indirectly, through their husbands. Although men assumed community leadership, vested in their councils, women in fact poured their thoughts into their husbands' ears. In many cases women would never voice their opinions in public, but privately their concerns reached their husbands and thereby influenced community decisions — provided that it was not something that affected specifically men's concerns.

Wives were indeed influential. No man would accept a job, decide to go on a long trip, or make any other important decision without first talking with his wife about it. After all, his gear, clothes, and other needs had to be in good shape before he left, and this might mean hours of work for his wife. As well, his wife had to live and be cared for while he was absent. He couldn't disregard her entirely and so, underground, the woman wielded a great influence in private and in community affairs. The men scornfully would say that they ignored the women's advice. But to gain the consent of a man to travel with you, it was necessary to have his wife's approval, though the man would never admit his wife had anything to do with it. This would be beneath his dignity.

In Eskimo life there was always need for a wife who, apart from normal duties, had to keep his clothes in repair so he wouldn't freeze on the trail. Men carry a little repair kit because often a major repair may be necessary, particularly if a man is away from home for a long time. Sewing is women's work, of course, but one must be practical. And Eskimo life was certainly that.

CHAPTER SIX

THE HIGHER QUESTIONS

MORAL LAW AND RETRIBUTION

Under Eskimo law, no man should ever kill a woman. Early in the century, there was a case in which an Eskimo employed by the police at Churchill killed his wife. For some reason, possibly for lack of evidence, the police exonerated him. But the Eskimos never allowed him to forget his crime. He himself told me about it after I'd seen him enter a house in which I was a guest. He ate alone and in silence without any other person making any attempt to speak to him. He told me that he was ostracized for having killed his wife (according to the Eskimos). Nevertheless, whenever he visited anyone he chose to, he had every right to have food placed before him, no matter what he had done. The laws of hospitality demanded this courtesy. The visit I witnessed took place some twenty or thirty years after the crime had supposedly been committed.

Shunning or ostracization was always the result of concerted action after a trial conducted by all the men of the community, and their decision was binding on all. In small hunting societies such as those of the Australian Aborigines, the Kalahari Desert Bushmen, or the Eskimos, being a full-fledged member of the group is critically important for a person's well-being. Conversely, because life is so interdependent in these small societies, shunning is usually a fate worse than death.

In another instance a boy crawling on the sea ice and hunting a seal was shot by his companion. The father of the dead boy claimed it was deliberate, and a week or two later, in an apparent accident, he shot the boy whom he blamed for his son's death. No one could prove murder, but the men of the community sat in council and decided that this man must be banished to a more southerly location and not be allowed to live and mingle with the rest of the tribe.

There have always been occasional, rare killings in the Arctic. In 1966, realizing that one of their members was seriously "bushed" or in a state of unbalanced mind and might be a menace to the community's security, all the men of the tribe met in conference and decided that the person in question should be removed. In such an emergency the community could choose one or two executioners to carry out the sentence, or all the men would act together. This they did years ago on Baffin Island, where the men half surrounded an igloo, inside which slept the killer of three; then they shouted to arouse him, simultaneously shooting into the igloo and killing the man. This occurrence wasn't reported to the police at the time, as it was considered tribal responsibility and not the concern of the white men.

Actually, that case indeed was the responsibility of the white men, who had ignored it. The person had been mentally unbalanced, treated in the white man's land, and then returned to his people without any controls. Surely, the Eskimos reasoned, the white man's point of view was inadequate, in that there was no protection of the community from this man, and so circumstances forced the Eskimos to take action.

On the other hand, temporary emotional upsets were always dealt with sympathetically. For example, an old man had only one son, and this son died. In his grief the old man became violent. The men of the community subdued him and tied him to the tent poles, where he could do no harm to others or himself. They fed him and cared for him with loving hands, and when three or four days later he was released, no stigma was attached to his past actions. Indeed, I rather suspect there was some admiration for him and a new respect because of his great love for his son.

A man's relationship with another man was his own private concern as long as other members of the community weren't involved. Perhaps one Eskimo wanted another man's wife, and all the people in the community knew about it. They could hardly not know of such domestic situations, because nothing was hidden in their small Arctic communities. Nobody would take any steps to do anything but, as elsewhere, a situation of this kind would be received with great interest. The community would hold that a man trying to take away the other man's wife would be known to the husband, that he, the husband, should accordingly be prepared for trouble and take action and kill the intruder before he himself was killed. The outcome of such a private matter wasn't to be interfered with by the tribe. The woman would become the wife of the survivor.

In another case, a man told an acquaintance whom he met on the trail that he was going to get a woman, the wife of a certain hunter, and if this acquaintance wanted to come along he could have the daughter. The second man declined the offer, but it was he who graphically told me just what happened. Arriving at the victim's igloo at daylight, the man kicked in the ice window, shot the sleeping husband, and forced the widow to accompany him. He got on his sled and made off with his prize and the seventeen-year-old daughter. The Eskimos considered this matter to be a private one, not the concern of the community.

Community decisions were made by Eskimo councils. These were composed of all the men of the tribe, including any male youths who were considered men. The council assembled in a tent or igloo, and the oldest man or the community leader would usually speak first on various subjects. In turn, the men would say what they thought about issues; anyone could speak his mind and agree or disagree. No changes could be made after the decision had been reached. Tribal decisions took precedence over all others, but the right of the individual to disagree was always upheld. In such meetings the younger men seldom spoke, but those who attended listened to the older members, because the Eskimos held that the elderly spoke sage advice; in this way age was venerated.

There was an exception to this rule in the leader of the community. A leader was a man who was a good hunter and provider, not only for himself and his family, but for those who had not. He was also able to organize and advise on the hunting tactics of others. Leaders never inherited their position. If a hunter was considered a leader, he was respected as such and his opinions carried great weight. Perhaps he became old and no longer provided as much as in the past, in which case another would gradually assume the position he had held. This progression was quite acceptable to the community. The best man would become leader and the former leader would assume second place. This involved no loss of face or respect; he'd done his best for the community, and now someone else could help in a better way. Whatever was best for the tribe was most important.

Where a group of people were gathered (and this was

determined by the abundance of available food), the old, suc-cessful hunter would often remain in his tent and send out the young men to bring in caches on fine days or to hunt the far reaches. Almost like some ancient potentates, the old men would sit in their tents or igloos and quietly give orders to the younger men, orders that were immediately obeyed. The very walk, stance, and commanding voice of these older men spoke volumes for their leadership.

Such men greatly influenced the life of the tribe, for in them rested the unwritten law of the Eskimo people and the lore of their country, handed down from father to son and leader to community. This manner of outlook and leadership made it very difficult for Eskimos to understand the white man's ways of choosing leaders, wherein people apply for a job which is awarded to the man who talks most about him-self. The Eskimo finds this inappropriate, because to him the braggart is not the kind of man needed.

CONJURORS AND TABOOS

In every Eskimo community there were angakoks (shamans or conjurors), persons of power and prestige in the com-munity. They were feared among the people because they were said to have control over the spirits, and thus had great influence over the whole community. Angakoks, both men and women, banded together in a lodge and supported one another in their controls over the community itself. The num-ber in any one given community could range from one to thirty, depending on the size of the community and the number of its members who had gone through the initia-tion rites, wherein the would-be angakok is instructed by an older shaman. The initiate, having gone through the rites, joined the community of angakoks. They had their own special language, understood only by the angakoks and not used in normal, everyday situations. Often new members would be quite young when they began lessons in learning this language.

The initiation of an angakok involved the person's going out on the land in isolation, to live alone for a long period without eating. Toward the end of this vigil, a "familiar spirit" would come to the initiate and attach itself to the anga-kok-elect for the rest of that person's life. Perhaps it's not quite correct to say for the rest of his or her life, because as

Adgekart, or "Floursack," the elder brother of Sam, was an outstanding and revered leader and benefactor whose great influence extended over a large area of Padlimiut territory. His wife was a shaman and his oldest son, Pommeook, was in training to become a shaman. He is wearing sun-goggles, usually made of willow, which were very important to prevent snow-blindness. A taboo forbade women and girls to wear them.

one angakok who became a Christian said, "When I became a Christian the power of the spirit was gone and never came back."

After this period of trial by living alone, some angakoks have done rather spectacular things to show the rest of the community that they are in communion with the spirits. For instance, one new angakok was taken to a lake in the middle of winter by an older shaman, who cut a hole in the ice and buried the body of the new angakok under the ice, where he was left for eight days. When the hole was reopened, he was brought back still alive.

The Eskimos tell of another very well known angakok on the west side of Hudson Bay who had the ability to make walrus tusks grow from his jaw. The Eskimos all claimed to have seen these tusks grow and described them in detail, even though many of these people had never seen a walrus; yet they were quite sure that the angakok had this ability. The tusks didn't just suddenly appear but grew from the jaw and became larger and larger. One of the white traders asked the angakok to allow him to take pictures of this remarkable sight, and the man agreed, with the proviso that no artificial light was to be used. Since the tusks appeared only at night in the dimness of the tent, the angakok could almost guarantee that no picture could be taken.

One Eskimo described to me what he considered to be a strange event relating to an angakok who lived on the northwestern side of Hudson Bay. The angakok went inside a tent, while people were scattered around on the outside waiting to see what would happen. Presently there was a tremendous noise inside, such as two people fighting or struggling fiercely, and then from underneath the skirt of the tent blood flowed out, at first in a trickle and then in a stream. Everyone immediately imagined the angakok to be fighting with the spirits, and the groaning they heard convinced them that he was being killed. After a while the groaning died away, and presently the angakok appeared looking very sleepy, as if he'd just awakened after conquering the spirit. When the Eskimos were invited into the tent, they saw blood on the floor but could see no other evidence of a battle or another being. This scene was rather typical of those that angakoks conjured, and one wonders sometimes about the truth of their claims.

Many angakoks wore signs of their craft on their backs. One man I knew always wore a harness like a dog's, in which he was said to be under the control of the spirits. Most angakoks wore a rope at their waists to which were attached pieces of skin and cloth; these materials were given them by people who were sick or who sought help from the angakok. The angakok would take a piece of cloth or animal skin from the patient, tear it in half, return half to the patient and wear the other half as his or her own, thus taking away the sickness from the patient. Amulets and charms were very often worn by them; perhaps the most common of these was the weasel skin, indicating great cunning which issued from the animal to the angakok. They might also wear pieces of sinew, which were said to give the angakoks great strength. Often they would sew the heart of a fish or that of a small animal into a little bag, attaching it inside the attigi on the breast or sewing it onto a child's bonnet to ensure protection and longevity.

For their treatment of sickness or for their professional advice the angakoks were paid with some of the most prized parts of animals, with skins or some article of clothing which

Floursack's wife (at left) and her friends gather last-minute items from the summer campsite in preparation for the fall migration. As an angakok or shaman, she wears her belt of office, a rope around the waist from which hang strips of cloth and skin given to her by patients to protect them from disease and ill fortune. Her summer coat, of white and navy blue pure wool "stroud," was particularly beautiful.

they particularly desired, or in some cases with sexual favours.

A shaman's job in the community was really to pronounce taboos and rules of conduct and ensure that they were well kept. Taboos were general behavioural prohibitions that applied to certain categories of people — such as women, pregnant women, or people who lived in certain locations. Other rules and prohibitions were applied to specific people according to various problems they might have or illnesses they might have incurred. Taboos were laid down literally by the thousands. Almost every act in life had a taboo or prohibition connected with it and, of course, it was almost certain that someone would inadvertently break one of them. For the breaking of taboos the angakoks laid down punishments (which could be quite remunerative for the angakok), but the gravest and most serious offences were those which were made by and affected the community at large and the people in it. It was thought that the spirits would be greatly upset by taboos being broken and that they would punish the community as a whole. Because the Eskimos felt that the community was more important than any individual, an infraction was a very serious matter.

The power of the angakoks was absolute. In one case an Eskimo had upset an angakok's sister. The shaman simply told him to rig up his rifle on top of his sled, muzzle facing toward himself, and lash it securely. He was to loop a string from the trigger over the back bar of the sled, lie down on the sled facing the gun and pull the cord. The man obeyed quickly, for he'd been told he must do it by the angakok himself. Needless to say, he killed himself.

Besides the numerous spirits that governed the ordinary angakok, there were two main spirits, one the spirit of the sea and the other the spirit of the land. Sedna, Goddess of the Sea, controlled all the sea mammals. Her story tells of a man and his daughter who went out to sea in a boat. A storm befell them, and water began to flood into the boat. To lessen the weight in the sinking vessel, the man threw his daughter overboard. She clung to the side of the boat and the man, in fear that he too would drown, took an axe and chopped off the first joints of her fingers, which became little seals. He then chopped off the next finger joints, and they became the bearded seals, and then the next, down to the knuckles, which became the walruses. After this, the daughter sank down into the water, where she became Sedna, Goddess of the Sea.

It was Sedna who created the storms on the sea; correspondingly, the Goddess of the Land created storms over the land. Anyone who has been in the Arctic and experienced an Arctic storm can appreciate the fury embraced in the winds across the Barren Lands and the Arctic Ocean.

Many Eskimo beliefs about clothing and hunting were related to the goddesses of sea and land, who must never be offended. For example, if you were wearing caribou-skin clothing when you came from the interior to the coast, it could never be sewn at the coast if ripped, and the front fringing of caribou skin had to be removed; otherwise Sedna would be offended and cause poor hunting and starvation for the people. On the other hand, if you were wearing seal-skin clothing and went inland and tore part of the sealskin, it couldn't be repaired until you returned to the coast.

The Eskimos, being animists, have always believed that lakes, lands, hills, and stones can be inhabited by spirits. In early days, a large stone not far from Eskimo Point was encircled by a sealskin rope on which were hung tins, kettles, pieces of cloth, strips of skin, and other goods, all of them offerings from the Eskimos to the spirit living in the stone.

Marble Island, not very far from Chesterfield, was said to have a spirit of its own. The stone of this island is white; when it appeared to turn black, the god was angry, and when it was white in the sunshine, the god was happy. One white trader laughed at the Eskimos for this belief, whereupon they warned him that he shouldn't upset the god. He went ashore at Marble Island at the same time as the Eskimos, all of whom knelt and said a prayer to the god. The trader took a few steps, slipped, and badly tore both knees, confirming to the Eskimos that there must be a god who was punishing him for not kneeling before it.

Among the many spirits that wandered about the land was one evil spirit who waited to steal people. So great was the fear of this spirit that even a grown man, a renowned and fearless hunter who normally would have no hesitation in killing a bear with only his knife, would be too afraid to venture on the land alone. He would always take a child or a second person with him. One Eskimo ran twenty miles across the land and arrived almost exhausted at the post, saying that he had seen this spirit, lying asleep next to a woman he had

A little girl at Eskimo Point wears a ragged parka, the neckline torn and rotted from her drooling and her runny nose. There is a taboo against fixing at the coast caribou clothing that had been worn inland and so, though it provides but poor protection from the cold, the parka may not be repaired.

stolen. The Eskimo was terrified and swore that what he'd seen was true, and he certainly believed it, because he'd left his dog team behind at the spot where he'd seen the woman and the devil.

Prohibitions and taboos were many. I once saw a woman whose baby was only three or four weeks old. Though the baby was adored, the mother simply had no concept of cleanliness; her coat was torn and ragged, dirty with filth, and the pouch at her back was soaked from the little one who slept there. I was horrified to see part of a little naked body peep through a tear in her pouch. The baby was blue from the cold, for the temperature was well below minus thirty degrees. I offered the mother some tea and suggested that the baby be warmed. She refused. For an Eskimo to refuse tea was almost unheard of. At last the story came out. For years she had wanted a baby, and finally one had arrived. She was overjoyed, but the angakok told her that to ensure that she didn't incur the wrath of the spirits who might harm the child, she must not eat anything made, handled, or touched by any white man, nor sew her garments, nor eat certain portions of the caribou. The effects of these particular prohibitions upon the little child almost broke my heart.

On one of my journeys westward into the interior, we came to an igloo where the Eskimos came out and welcomed us and invited us in as usual. I shook hands with them at the front of the long opening then went down a tunnel into the igloo proper. There a young mother asked me if I had any milk with me, and I told her I hadn't, because I don't carry milk on the trail. When I asked her why she wanted the milk she replied, "Because my baby is starving." She was seated on the snow bench, and from the pouch at the back of her coat she took out a little morsel of humanity, whose arms were no thicker than a broomstick and whose skin hung loosely like gossamer. I asked her what had happened, and she said, "Well, my husband went out one day to hunt and he saw a wolf. He shot the wolf but didn't kill it, and so he took an axe and killed it. In doing this he broke some of its bones, and this is taboo." As a result of this violation, she explained, she wasn't allowed to eat certain parts of caribou because he had broken the taboo. Then she went on, "My husband became very sick." (From the description of the sickness, I'm sure he had developed pneumonia.) The angakok told her that her husband was sick because the spirits were angry. He died, and as a result of his death, certain other parts of the caribou became taboo for her to eat because of the taboos operative at death. Then the baby was born, and even more taboos regarding food became operative, and now she simply said, "I just have no milk to feed my baby." She

Aoledgoot makes a poignant plea for milk to feed her starving baby.
Because of various taboos about what she could and could not eat, her
diet had become so restricted that her milk had dried up. Donald took
her and her baby back to Eskimo Point, where they were able to save the
child from death.

said she had taken bannock (bread made of flour, baking powder, and lard), chewed it in her mouth, moistened it with black tea, and pushed it into her child's mouth.

We traveled seventy miles back to the post (with me running ahead of the dog team) and took the mother and child with us. Two days later, with some thirty-six hours of traveling behind us, we arrived at the mission station very early in the morning. We saved the baby, but for six weeks the child didn't have the strength even to suck. The mother continued to feed it mouth to mouth and then gradually with a medicine dropper. The mother, though she loved the child, would never have broken the taboos on her own, but she was indeed grateful for the care and attention we gave her child. This child lived because we had heard of the need, but many others didn't.

Snow goggles were another taboo for women. It's a sad sight to see a little five-year-old girl rubbing red-rimmed, weeping eyes with a grubby fist, her red cheeks swollen and almost raw from the eye discharge, and to watch her stumbling along over the rocks almost unable to see her way, especially when you realize that if she had been a boy she could have worn wooden goggles. Being a woman, however, albeit a very young one indeed, she must suffer.

It wasn't an uncommon sight in early days to see a boy wearing girl's clothing with braided hair tied at the back of the head with bits of fur. Even his name would have been changed, all in the hope of fooling the spirits. The boy would have been the only son left in a large family (which could well have had twenty or twenty-four births), and it was vitally necessary that the spirits, who had caused the death of the other boys, should be fooled into thinking that this was a girl. Girls, after all, had little intrinsic value, and a spirit would hardly bother itself to hurt one. If the spirit weren't fooled, perhaps the many charms on the breast of the parka and across the shoulders and the small of the back would ward off evil, and the number of these charms indicated how concerned the parents were for the welfare of their only living son.

In spite of these and other tales it should be understood that angakoks were not always deliberate deceivers nor simply conjuring tricksters; they believed in their powers, which originated in the spirits. Many taboos were created by them for the sake of the people, rather like our laws, whereby certain rules are laid down for the good of the community.

DEATH

Sometimes tragedy strikes quickly and violently in the Arctic, and at other times death comes slowly, agonizingly. Perhaps starvation has taken its toll. A pile of household goods and bits of personal belongings scattered among a few bones are mute evidence to the finder that another family has passed out of the picture. In time of starvation old people who knew they were a burden to a family that had to move quickly in their search for food might order their son or son-in-law to build an igloo where the old person would be walled in to die, while the rest of the family set out on the long trek in hope of survival.

In as vast a land as the Canadian North, those who become lost, who fail to make the grade or surmount the demands of their harsh environment, are never seen alive again. But when death comes in the ordinary way to a camp or igloo, time-honoured customs prevail.

Adgekart and his relatives were camped on the rise of the beach at Eskimo Point in the early spring of 1926. His son, who had been ill for some time, lay dying. Without speaking everyone in turn took his hand in theirs in final farewell. Suddenly, harsh and shrill wailing came from the tent; the young man was dead. Relatives came one by one to fill the tent, each new arrival a signal for another outburst of grief. The father sat dry-eyed and tight-lipped, stunned by the realization that his only son had left him. Women relatives spoke in undertones as they consulted Adgekart, who directed that his son be buried on the hill located about a mile across the sea ice. There his forefathers had camped and a relative had once been buried.

Every summer camping site was in a place where there were plenty of boulders to hold down tent skirts, and stone rings were common across the land. Families usually returned every year to the same place until there was a death in the family or community, when the site would be abandoned for at least five years and not used again unless it was really necessary. On the height of land on Hudson Bay's western side, such sites had been used for centuries. Adgekart's son would be buried in one of these places.

The women relatives collected all that had belonged to the dead young man — his clothes, tools, rifle, harpoon, pipe, tobacco, and cup — and placed them all together in a pile. Then they dressed the dead boy in his best clothes, covering him with his new beaded coat, which he'd never worn. All this happened amid the renewed wailing of his mother and wife and the cries of the little ones who clung to their skirts. Suddenly the mother caught the dead boy to herself and cried for him to come back. Passionately she held him and rubbed noses. Only then did his father's reserve break, and he too sobbed and wailed.

Meanwhile, the women had taken skins from the sleeping bench and placed a large one on the ground. On it they put the boy's everyday garments. Finally they laid the body down and placed more deerskins on top. At the head on the left side were placed his pipe filled with tobacco, matches, and a mug of water. These were for his use when making the long journey to the land of life after death. To the accompaniment of renewed wailing the deerskin coverings were lashed, and the corpse passed through a hole cut in the back of the tent, a custom practised to deceive the spirits, who would no longer remain in the dwelling to harm the surviving occupants. The opening was quickly repaired to appear as usual. Six women, walking three on each side, carefully carried the bundle to his sled, together with all his belongings, and then began their trek across the sea ice. No men accompanied them. It's taboo for a man to touch a dead body or for a man to build a grave. Above all, anything upon which the body rested could never be used again.

At the grave site the women gathered rocks, knocking each stone loose from the frozen ground. They had chosen a flat spot on a rise. They laid the body with the head toward the west and carefully built a stone cairn around it. They inclined an upright pole toward the west, away from the head, to signify that a man or boy was here. A pole slanted toward the north denoted a woman or girl.

Graves were of two kinds, open or covered. In the former, the body was laid on the ground, wrapped in deerskins, and encircled by fairly large stones. With the covered type of grave, a cairn was erected, the walls of which resembled those of a house. Pieces of wood — or in the case of a man, his sled or canoe paddles — were laid across the walls and then covered with large slabs of stone. Spaces between stones were carefully filled with smaller stones, moss, or soil. Stones of white quartz placed at the head denoted a distinctive custom followed for all graves. In some cases stones were quite large and used as supports for an old stone pot or blubber lamp. Some graves on Southampton Island have a long slab of stone for the bottom and are lined with white stones, with another pile placed at the head. A Padlimiut woman told my wife that the white stones were there to let in light.

After a death, for five days the women visited the grave, to sit and talk for hours with the spirit of the deceased, believing it still lingered somewhere in the region of the body. Eskimos' old beliefs included the view that when good people died, they went upward to the moon, encountering various

145

stages as they progressed into greater and greater light. At the first stage, the deceased played ball continually with a walrus head. Very thin clothes were believed to be worn at the second stage, one of increasing brightness; at this stage there would be plenty of seals and caribou, and a sled that bridged a crevasse allowed the animals to get to a den. The third stage contained a very bright place with an abundance of food. Everyone there was thought to be extraordinarily happy. It was believed that there were many people living at this place close to the moon. Bad people remained in their shrouds, however, surrounded by many fighting spirits.

At burial time not only the immediate family, but the whole community was subject to strict taboos. Hunting, sewing, eating, and many other aspects of life were affected. Kootneak's daughter, for example, gave birth to a baby girl who lived for only ten days. The body of the child was sewn into deerskins and laid next to the mother on the snow bench. There it lay for five days. During this time the mother was not allowed to dress or eat certain foods. Kootneak was an angakok who rigidly enforced old customs and taboos. Years later, after his son Amaroogyooak was wonderfully delivered from death, old Kootneak changed and eventually embraced Christianity.

Tragedy fell upon us at Eskimo Point one winter. On a Sunday morning, Amaroogyooak, together with two slightly older lads, set out by dog team to bring home some meat from their caches. Each of his two companions also had a dog team. Out on the Barrens, as so often happens in the North, a blizzard blew up within a few minutes, and by evening it was impossible to see beyond a few feet. The boys had gone forth poorly equipped for such a night. They had no sleeping robes and only a primus lamp. For food, they had only frozen caribou from the cache. The oldest boy had built an igloo, and so they were safe for the night.

Two days later the oldest arrived back at the post. His companions had been lost in the blizzard. This boy had the best team, with eight dogs, whereas the others had but six and three. Amaroogyooak had only the three poor dogs. Consternation in camp was great, but it was impossible to search for the lost ones until the blizzard weakened. On the next day the snow was driving and swirling to heights of eight feet or more. It was impossible to see more than twelve yards away. Several teams left the post under the command of the RCMP natives, but they returned after a fruitless search. On the fourth day the search continued, but still there was no news. Then someone saw what seemed to be a phantom coming through the swirling snow, three weary dogs battling against the wind and a person sitting motionless on the sled, his deerskin clothing sticking out like a hoop skirt, frozen solid. People rushed from all directions. Questions flew at the motionless figure. He replied abruptly, and slowly, painfully, he stood up. Amaroogyooak was back.

Later we learned of the first night, when all three boys had slept together in an igloo. On the next morning the oldest boy had insisted on their going home. In the drifts he had lost Amaroogyooak and his companion. They were both terribly afraid, especially when darkness descended and they were wrapped in the pitiless blizzard, with whirling pieces of snow cutting their faces and merciless cold gripping their bodies. They had no shelter. They simply dropped down upon their upturned sleds. The other boy was the beloved firstborn of Elekoot. He had fine, beautifully patterned deerskin clothing, but he seemed to feel the cold more than Amaroogyooak, even though the latter had much poorer clothing. So Amaroogyooak gave the only deerskin they had to his companion to lie on and, folding his arms across his chest and inside his coat, he lay down in the snow.

Dawn came at last. The other boy seemed drowsy, and Amaroogyooak had to kick him awake. Both boys had been without food for two days. Another day passed the same as the last, with them both battling to make their way home. A night came and went as well. They cried, and who could blame them? The next morning Amaroogyooak's dogs were so weak they couldn't keep up with the other team. So Amaroogyooak was left behind. He spent a night alone. Cold and hungry, he prayed for help and cried. On the next day he arrived at the post, having been lost for four days.

In the wake of his arrival, teams went out to scour the land around the post, for surely the other boy must be close at hand. Nevertheless, by the time it was dark he was still lost. The blizzard finally ended. All was calm and still. Then, panic-stricken, everyone joined in the search. Little twinkling lights went bobbing across the snow, carried by men, either running or on sleds, who kept crying out, hoping to hear an answering howl from the lost boy's dogs. Lights were hoisted to the top of the police radio pole and on the highest building. A beacon flashed from the top of a small rise.

It was now one o'clock. The night was so still, so quiet. Then there came a different cry from the south, coming closer. They had found the boy at last, frozen to death just a mile from home. There would be another burial.

CHAPTER SEVEN
MAKING DO

The Eskimos live in a hard country that yields its treasures meagrely at times and often at great cost, so they had to become extremely cautious of a sometimes fickle environment but also be loremasters of that same environment. They needed thorough knowledge of the possibilities offered by their environment, which in turn required a creative spirit and careful observation in the smallest things, just to survive.

I remember speaking to an Eskimo one day about spiders, as he'd seen me collect specimens for the Royal Ontario Museum. He proceded to tell me not only about the varieties of spiders, but also how they mate, catch their prey, and eat; in short, a complete life history. In reply to my question as to how he knew all this, he said, "Oh, I spent a whole day once not even eating, but just watching a spider."

Their detailed knowledge of how any animal of the North lives, what it eats, and how it survives is a composite history created out of an individual's careful watchfulness as well as from traditions handed down from previous generations. There is an inquisitiveness to know which seems to be inherent in every Eskimo. Matching this inquisitiveness into the nature of things is an ability to make the most of each season wherever the Eskimo is in the Arctic. Perhaps he adapts himself to the Arctic environment, but then again, perhaps he adapts the Arctic environment to himself!

During late spring and summer some of the inland Eskimos, essentially caribou hunters, resided at the coast in order to enjoy the advantages of hunting sea mammals such as seal and walrus. Others lived all year round a little north of Eskimo Point and combined sea and land cultures.

There was usually considerable excitement in the camp when the round head of a seal, rather resembling a football afloat, popped up in the sea. The size of the head determined whether the quarry was a square flipper, a freshwater, or a common seal. A kayak or canoe is necessary to hunt seals, and an Eskimo in his kayak in earlier times could easily out-manoeuvre a seal, provided it hadn't become too wary. When harpooned by the hunter, the seal would dart off towing an inflated sealskin float attached to the harpoon. Eventually the seal would tire, then the Eskimo could paddle close to the seal, lance it, and haul it on board.

The Eskimos most enjoyed sealing in the springtime, for then the seals lie on top of the ice, every now and again raising their heads to look around for enemies and then dozing in the warm sunshine. The hunter, using as camouflage a shield of whitened sealskin with a peephole in the centre, was able to crawl unobserved within killing range of his prey.

The Caribou Eskimo seldom, if ever, went out with a dog in the middle of winter to search for seal holes, as did their more northerly neighbours, nor did they stand on the sea ice in the middle of winter with harpoon poised, waiting for the breath of a seal to disturb the fine piece of swansdown suspended over a hole, again as their northern neighbours did. They did, however, use a dog in the springtime to sniff out seal holes and to find under them the cavern in which a young seal would lie while its mother left to hunt. Having found the hole, the hunter would suddenly jump on top of it with all his weight, throwing out his arms to make sure he wouldn't fall through. The ice that fell in would trap the

A hunter draws a seal through a hole in the ice after he has harpooned it. Sometimes he must wait hours at the hole for such a prize, and there is never a guarantee he will bag a meal, as seals often use more than one breathing hole. More than likely, however, he used one of his dogs to sniff out the quarry, and this takes considerably less time.

young seal and sometimes the mother as well. Both would be quickly dispatched. The little white sealskin pelt would make a warm coat or hat for his baby.

The seal, once taken home, was put to many uses, which is where the women's work came in. Sometimes the adult seal was skinned by removing meat and bones through its mouth, thus leaving the whole skin intact. Then a woman would turn the skin inside out, scrape it free of fat, inflate it with air by blowing into it, and tie it onto a skin line to dry. Later her husband would use it as a float while hunting sea mammals.

Sealskin line was made by cutting a long strip in a spiral around the outer skin of a whole seal carcass in widths of

Kownuk removes the fat from a sealskin while her son is busy flensing and her little daughter searches for tidbits. The fat will be stored in a dan (sealskin bag) for winter use either with caribou meat or in a blubber lamp.

151

about one-half to three-quarters of an inch. This line was then stretched out and allowed to dry on the ground, with bones driven into the ground to hold it taut. Later on, if necessary, a woman chewed or worked the line to soften it before use as a whip, rope, lash, or for tying things to a sled.

Generally, however, the skin was removed by cutting from the throat right down to the tail. When flesh, bones, and fat had been cut out, the skin was flensed, with the whole skin pegged out on the ground to dry. If the skin was needed without hair for boot bottoms, it was thrown into fresh water and allowed to rot so that the hair could be removed with an ulu. If a waterproof skin was needed, the black pelt covering the skin on the outside was left on and only the hair removed. For fancy sealskin boots, dehaired skins were hung up on a pole in winter and left in the fierce glare of the sun to bleach completely white.

The seams of sealskin boots were made waterproof by double sewing, a method in which the seams were overlapped and the skilful stitching on each side did not go completely through the skin, but only halfway in each flap, thus allowing no water to penetrate. A pair of sealskin or bearskin pants were of great value, because they were waterproof and protected a man in the springtime if he slid on his seat as he hunted on the sea ice — which was covered with pools of water by that time of year.

Either the flesh was used at once for human and dog food, or someone would cache the whole carcass under rocks for use later in the year, primarily as dog food, even though it might be very "high" in smell and taste. For Eskimos who relied on seal oil for their lamps, blubber from the seal served well. The blubber was often cut into small pieces and pounded with a stone to release the oil from it; this fed the moss wicks along the edge of the blubber lamp, or koodluk, which gave light and some heat within the igloo.

Until about 1960 sealskins were never really part of the trade economy, because they were used mainly by the Eskimos for clothing and food; they took the place of cloth and provided materials that the Eskimos needed within their own economy. The outside world in general didn't consider sealskins as furs and so was not particularly interested in them. The sealing season continued until the ice moved out of the bay, when dog teams could no longer cross the rotting ice

In the springtime hunters almost daily took their dogs across the ice to the floe edge to hunt seals in Hudson Bay. Often their canoes were lashed to the sled. The sun's rays melt the surface snow, leaving pools and lagoons of remarkably pure drinking water upon the surface of the sea ice. Crossing the fast-rotting sea ice was precarious business. Hunters usually waited until after sundown, when the water iced over, to return to camp. Break-up usually occurred by the end of June, and then sealing days were over until next year.

to the floe edge. By that time spring break-up had officially arrived.

Skins of most animals played important roles in the lives of Eskimos. Though some skins were more highly prized than others, the species used for various purposes depended largely on the kinds and number of animals available for hunting in the various areas. Caribou, of course, were abundant at times. The same spiral method used to cut sealskin line was used in making caribou-skin line, though this was sometimes also cut from a skin laid out flat. The line, when dried and made pliable, was useful for dog harnesses and traces, for lashing tents and sleds, and as an anchor rope to tether boats. The skin of the large bearded seal was greatly prized because it was both strong and thick, far stronger than ordinary sealskin line, but not so thick as to be unmanageable. Walrus line was hard to handle and heavy in weight.

But seal, caribou, and walrus lines were usually too thick and unbending for many purposes, and a thinner, more pliable twine was needed. The sinew from the leg of a caribou was greatly valued as twine because it could be plaited into a jigging line used to catch fish, into laces for boots, or into a line for general binding and lashing. The back sinew of the caribou served a multitude of purposes; for example, heads of tools could be bound with sinew onto shafts, and the sinew served as thread for sewing shoes, clothing, and tents. In springtime, when the surface of the snow became slippery, knotted and plaited sinew or thin knotted sealskin or caribouskin line sewn onto the bottoms of boot soles ensured that the wearer wouldn't slip or fall easily. Sinew was also used for a kind of household cement: any cracked bone or broken article of wood, stone, bone, or antler could be pierced on each side of the split or crack and lashed firmly with sinew.

Many lengths of sinew went into an Eskimo hunting bow. The three to five pieces of caribou antler used for the structure of the bow itself were either riveted together with native copper or bound carefully with wet sinew line and allowed to dry. A stiff backing of plaited sinew of many thicknesses was placed along the front edge of the bow and lashed to it, greatly strengthening it. Then a plaited sinew string was stretched out and tied end to end, completing the bow.

Arrow tips were of stone, flint, antler, or whalebone (later iron) and were bound to a shaft of willow wood or antler. These were retrieved whenever possible, of course, to be used again and again. Harpoons also were made of caribou antler.

In the 1920s Eskimo children used crossbows in hunting. I was never able to find out if men ever used them for hunting; the reply when I asked how the children had learned to make and use crossbows invariably was, "Oh, our grandfathers taught us how to make them."

Hunting methods and techniques, of course, were handed down from father to son. One method that children could practise at an early age was the stone trap, wherein a vertical stick stood on top of a piece of meat and also supported a heavy, flat rock, all of which rested above a slight depression in the ground. If a fox happened to tug at the meat, the heavy stone would drop down on top of him and hold him powerless. This method was similar in principle to the trap that little boys set by spreading crumbs or meat for birds under a similarly heavy stone, except that the stick was tied to a piece of string held by a motionless hunter some distance away. When the birds lost fear and started to feed, the hunter yanked the cord at the appropriate moment, trapping one or more birds under the stone.

As in other parts of the world besides the Arctic, a bolas was used to hunt birds and small animals. Three bones of equal size and weight were each fastened to one end of three pieces of plaited sinew about twelve inches long. The three cords were then knotted together at the other end, and the simple weapon was complete. If a bird happened to be seen running along the ground (in the spring birds are often unable to fly easily), the weapon was deftly rotated by holding one of the bones and whirling the thing around one's head. When released the bolas whirled at great speed. If one's aim were true, the swirling bolas wrapped itself around the legs or body of the bird and brought it to the ground. The hunter would run forward to catch the bird before it could disentangle itself and escape.

But times bring inevitable changes. I remember an experience at the mission house during the fall of 1940. "What are those?" asked an Eskimo boy, indicating a set of harpoon heads that had been found near an old grave on an island just off the western shore of Hudson Bay. I thought this young man of some twenty years was fooling, but his three companions assured me that none of them knew what they were. I explained that variously sized and shaped harpoon heads were used to kill different animals, such as walrus or bearded seal or ordinary seal. They laughed and said I was trying to fool them. It wasn't until an old Eskimo came in that they believed me.

My thoughts then went back some seventeen or eighteen years earlier, when I'd watched an Eskimo rub away at a solid block of iron with an old, worn file that had decrepit teeth, to file a harpoon head. I asked how long he'd worked on it.

"Three days."

"How long yet before it will be finished?"

"Another three or four days."

Here was not only a piece of art — if I may call it that — but a monument to the patience that was typical of the Eskimo people. Harpoons of that type were used by Eskimos living around the coast of the Arctic islands.

Muzzle loaders had made early inroads in the Far North, and it was common even until 1930 to see them used for the hunt. Muzzle loaders were often dangerous to use, and sometimes one heard of accidents. I know of several Eskimos with faces badly scarred from an overburst of a gun that had been too full with a charge of powder. Sometimes one would find on the ground powder horns that had been bought at the store by some hunter in the past. One could see on the wooden plug the hunter's teeth marks, left from repeatedly gripping the stopper with his teeth to pull it out, so that powder could be tipped into the hand and later into the muzzle loader.

Snow or ice down the muzzle of a rifle or gun could burst the barrel if it was fired. The fur clothes of the Eskimos provided a plug of hair used to keep the muzzle clear. In the age of muzzle loaders and even today, hair could be rammed down the muzzle to hold the charge and ball in place. Back in 1926 at Churchill, a white hunter was out on his traplines and saw a silver fox worth about $150 (a lot of money in those days). He had no wad for his muzzle loader and nothing with which to ram home the charge. Suddenly he remembered a fifty-dollar bill in his pocket. He quickly stuffed half of it into the gun on top of the powder, the other half on the bullet, rammed it home, and shot the fox. He later remembered that he could have used half the bill and collected the value of the other half, but he made a profit anyway.

The development of tools and weapons by the Eskimos depended in the early days on the materials close at hand from which articles could be fashioned. Stone cooking pots, blubber lamps, and pipes for smoking tobacco (after the white man's arrival) were made of soapstone, but because this was found only in certain areas, some of the Eskimos traded stone for various articles from other tribes. The soapstone lamps themselves were seldom traded, because each group had its own shape and size in both pots and lamps. For instance, the lamps of the people who lived at the north end of Bathurst Inlet in the western Arctic were often six feet long and really heavy (the owners loved warm houses). But the single most important factor in their use wasn't so much the availability of stone for making them as it was the fuel to burn in them. The scarcity or abundance of white whale, seal, walrus, or even fish determined the size of lamps and the kind of oil used to keep the lamps burning.

Fuel for fire was indeed scarce north of the tree line, and women had to spend hours collecting enough fuel (mosses, lichens, and willow twigs) for cooking. But since man's earliest days, fire has been one of the most important things in his life. It's superfluous to say that this is truer than ever in the Arctic. However, using frozen, raw meat for food, dipping water from an ice hole, and dressing in carefully made skin clothing, coupled with great care in not allowing oneself to get wet or perspire too heavily in winter, made it possible for Eskimos to live without fire in a country where we would consider it an absolute necessity.

But the Eskimos learned how to make and use fire, too. They developed the bow drill: a green stick braced in a small depression in a dry wooden board was rotated rapidly with a bow, the "string" of which was a thong of skin looped around the stick and pulled quickly backwards and forwards. One turn of the skin line around the drill forced it to rotate. With the aid of a mouthpiece the drill stick was kept in place, simultaneously allowing pressure to be applied as the drill was swiftly revolved first one way and then the other. The friction created on the board produced a spark, which ignited a pile of dried caribou moss and which, with the aid of a puff or two of breath, was kindled into flame. Then came the white man, who introduced flint and tinder, and later fuses (short matches), so that fire could be created more easily and in less time.

Far to the west of Hudson Bay in the Coppermine area, large deposits of copper can still be found lying free on the ground surface. For centuries the copper has been used by the Eskimos there. They found that they could pound it into new shapes and so make tools of copper, or they edged antler and horn, butting the edges with flattened copper. They became so expert in its use and nature that they could tell you where the copper came from by its texture alone, since the copper from various areas differs in density. Copper also served well for clamps or rivets to hold broken or cracked stone cooking pots together and proved an invaluable commodity for spring trading, which took place on the height of land between Hudson Bay and the West, at Hikolijuak.

In the western Arctic snow knives, women's knives,

Ayaranee using a bow drill to produce a spark.

chisels, and other goods were fashioned from copper, and
there a material culture developed, based on copper, which
differed substantially from that of the Caribou Eskimos and
also from that of the Eskimos on the Arctic archipelago.

The resourcefulness of Eskimos, all things considered,
seems endless. One lad, for example, watched with envy
another who owned a pair of skates. The next day he
appeared with his own specially designed "skates." He had
cut two strips of metal from a steel drum and driven each

strip into the wide side of a piece of two-by-four wood. Then he drove nails sideways into the wood, which enabled him to lash the makeshift skates on his feet with sealskin line. Soon he too was skimming over the ice.

To cite another, different example, the pads of a dog's feet can be badly cut on the ice in springtime, when the sun's rays cause the ice surface to "candle." To help prevent crippling the dogs, Eskimos made little boots from skin and tied them around the dogs' feet. Somehow most of the dogs knew enough not to bite them off on the trail.

While visiting in an igloo one day, I learned of an Eskimo's discovery. Between two igloos was a tautly stretched skin line, the ends of which were fastened to two empty coffee cans set in the snow wall inside each igloo. By shouting into the tin in one igloo, anyone in the other igloo could make out what was said. When I asked where he got the idea, the Eskimo simply replied that he'd thought it out for himself.

It was only inevitable that Eskimo resourcefulness and their love of good fun would combine and be formalized into regularly held activities. Though the winter held its share of offerings for homespun entertainment, it was the summer especially when the camps came alive.

Nooglooktok was a game for everybody. A piece of bone suspended on a line had a hole drilled in the middle of it. The object of the game was to spear the bone through the hole, using pointed sticks or lances. Here younger boys at Eskimo Point improve their skill at nooglooktok. Note the strings attached to both top and bottom of the bone to keep it taut but still guarantee rotation if the hole is missed.

Men of Eskimo Point combine the frustrations of nooglooktok with the thrill of gambling.

CHAPTER EIGHT

. . . AND
ENJOYING IT

GAMES

Springtime always heralded a period of celebration, feasting, and fun, for spring brought more than warmer weather and the thaw; many Eskimo families returned to Eskimo Point for the season's work — and play. Everyone participated, and the sorrows and tragedies of the past winter would be forgotten in the prospect of spring's renewal. The short summer season marked a period when hunting, fishing, cooking, sewing, and moss gathering assumed second priority to community pleasures. It was time to enjoy life.

Both men and women enjoyed the very popular gambling games. One of the most popular was nooglooktok. In it a group would squat around a tripod formed by three tent poles. Each person was armed with a short, arrow-like lance, a stick about two or three feet long with a sharpened file tied onto it to form the point. Suspended from the apex of the poles on a piece of skin line was a small, oblong piece of bone, its lower end strung to a piece of rock on the ground beneath to keep it tautly in position. The bone had a half-inch hole drilled through it. At a given signal all the players simultaneously poked their lances forward repeatedly at the hole. At each poke there was a staccato "click, click, click" sound, for every time anyone hit the bone, it spun rapidly on its vertical axis, making it even more difficult to spear the hole. This repetitive lunging would go on until at last one spear would find a home in the bone, and then the whole group would sit back and watch the winner take the prize, which would have been put up by the previous winner. The new winner would then have to put up something of his own for the next round's stakes. Sometimes it was a new rifle or an old, absolutely worthless piece of skin. But this was all part of the game. Winners were expected to put up some prize; it might be valuable or completely otherwise; it didn't

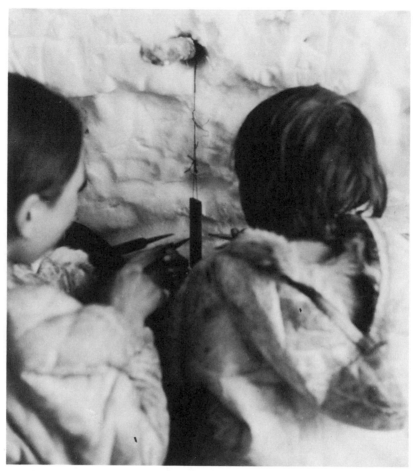

During winter, young children with toy spears would spend hours playing nooglooktok in their igloos.

matter. Men, women, and children played nooglooktok for the fun of playing and not just to win.

Eskimos also played the game of hiding an object in one hand behind the back, another person having to guess in which hand the object was hidden. If he or she guessed correctly, it would be that person's turn to take the object and hide it. This game was quickly over, needless to say, but it was repeated over and over and so gave an excellent opportunity for gambling.

Eskimo families also thoroughly enjoyed playing with

162

Children play a favourite game, "Store," within sheltering walls that they have made outside. Like children everywhere playing at being grown up, they imitate the trading transactions they have seen at the HBC store. Outdoor games are typically of short duration in the cold winter.

string and were adept at making cat's cradles of various kinds, many of them masterpieces of ingenuity and complexity, often just to amuse their children. Frequently one person would start a simple design and then pass the string to another person, who would have to add the next step in the design, with perhaps a new twist. The two would pass the string back and forth, each time progressively complicating the challenge and the design, until one of them could no longer think of another move. They were marvelously clever at thinking out, finishing, and making new designs. In some ways the game rivaled chess for its logic and intricacy.

The Padlimiut were also wonderful checker players and spent many long hours in the summertime playing it with one another in their tents, and in the wintertime in their igloos. Their rules were slightly different from ours, and they knew every move on the board, so they invariably beat a white man.

Playing cards were always of interest to the Eskimos; they played card games in which they matched cards rather than games in which they counted numbers on them. They also played a kind of solitaire, using a piece of bone with many holes bored in it and attached by a piece of sinew to a bone needle some three or four inches long. They would toss the pierced bone into the air and try to catch it on the needle. The Eskimos could almost always do this because of long practice; so the game also involved seeing whether or not one could say a piece of doggerel — one word each time the bone was impaled — or whether one could count up to twenty, impaling the bone on the needle every time. If there was a miss, the weighty bone would give the knuckles a sharp rap.

The children just loved to make and put cut-outs on igloo walls. They would cut out pieces of skin or pieces of paper into shapes and figures and then hold them against a damp snow wall. In a very short while the cut-out would be frozen in place, a speedy way to decorate the inside of an igloo. They also loved to play with dolls. Mother would make a bundle of skin and tie a bit of string around one end so that it resembled a head. Eskimo children would give tender love and care to these dolls; they would carry them in their parka hoods, talk to them and fuss over them, then put them to bed in the sleeping skins, differently from but also so like the way children treat dolls the world over.

In summertime the men and boys would stretch a sealskin rope horizontally at a height of some four or five feet from the ground, bracing it on the tent-pole tripod. On this rope the young Eskimos did all sorts of gymnastics or calisthenics — under, over, in and up — vying with one another in real feats of agility and strength. This activity continued during the winter in the igloo, especially when there were energetic male youths, although then the ends of the rope were passed outside the igloo itself and were looped around a stick or board to prevent the igloo's snow wall from being pulled in.

Men often held individual contests between themselves. In one of their versions of arm wrestling, each of two men held his forearm against the other's and, by pressing one against the other, each would try to force the other's arm down flat on the bench or table. This was a very common form of trial of strength, and often men were great rivals. But there were times when men got annoyed with each other, and then the two contestants would put their heads down and short punch each other on the temple as hard as they could. Obviously the winner was the one still standing at the end. But even what appeared to be fighting was done all in fun.

A little boy plasters cut-outs of skin or paper against an igloo wall.

THE DRUM DANCE

One afternoon in June, as I was walking among the tents, I happened to glance into Ootoroot's and noticed that he was busily absorbed in stretching a skin across the frame of an enormous drum. I entered and sat down at his side on the sleeping skins. He remarked, "The Eskimos are going to drum dance tonight. Come along and see us." Then for a few moments there was silence as he pulled the drum skin taut,

*Preparing the drum for a drum dance. Ootoroot stretches the skin to
tauten this large drum, which is tilted on its stubby handle.*

carefully stretching out every wrinkle in its surface. The
frame was made from a piece of willow that had been
steamed and bent into a circular shape about thirty inches in
diameter. The rim was something less than two inches thick
and had been grooved on the outside so that the string holding the skin in place would remain there. The handle was ten
inches long and round, with a groove in it about a third of
the way down. The rim of the drum fitted closely into this
groove, and sinew line bound the two together.

At last Ootoroot had the drum skin taut enough. He
remarked that the Eskimos were happy to be having a dance.
When I asked him what they did at the drum dance, he
replied, "You'll see tonight." Then while he searched for his
wife's sewing kit, he went on to tell me that every man has
at least one song, which the women sing while he dances.

Most of them have several songs and some Eskimos have as many as twenty or thirty. Having found the kit and a needle, he threaded it with a fine piece of sinew taken from the dried back muscle of a caribou. Then he carefully sewed a small patch of thin, almost transparent parchment over a small hole in the drum skin. While working he explained that this tissue came from the heart of a caribou, the only material suitable for repairing a drum skin because it didn't impair the drum's tone.

The sewing completed, Ootoroot took the tea kettle and, lifting it high in the air, drew a mouthful of water from the spout. He squirted water over the skin's surface, moving his head from side to side to ensure that the water was evenly spread over it. Taking a scraper with an iron blade, he proceeded to scrape the skin lightly until the whole surface had been treated. He treated the other side in the same way. This, he explained, would allow the skin to be stretched once more.

Using a piece of wood shaped like a marlin spike he began to tighten the drum skin, and as he did I asked him why he didn't ask his wife to sew the patch. "That," he replied, "must not be. A woman must not stretch or prepare the drum skin. No, it's not for religious reasons; this taboo has been handed down for generations, and so we carefully observe it to this day." Having by this time finished stretching the skin, Ootoroot carefully rolled the loose edges under a length of line which he wound around the drum.

I asked him what the songs of the Eskimos are about. There are four kinds of songs, he said, and any one man may have several of each in his repertoire. Every hunter composes his own songs and teaches them to his wife, who in turn teaches the other women; therefore, every woman knows the songs of every man in the tribe. Then with a smile Ootoroot explained that there are songs about white men, their peculiarities and oddities. (For instance, one man has a song in which he describes a missionary's wife: "She has a waist like a wasp and two front teeth like a walrus.")

A second type of song deprecates the ability of the hunter himself to obtain enough food for his family. (It's only the good hunters who have songs such as this.) A third type is much like the second; these songs tell that the hunter can't find enough food and has to eat food that other people give him. (Usually the owner of such a song always has plenty to eat and gives freely to others — basically the opposite of the situation described in the song.) The fourth type recounts the personal bravery of the drummer or tells of some long or famous trip that he has made in the past.

Ootoroot further explained that quite a young man may have many songs that were originally those of another person. This person was always a namesake and may have given the songs to the young man while he, the originator, was still alive.

The drum was now finished and Ootoroot carefully placed it at the back of the tent, remarking, "One of my sons will be telling the people when to come to dance, and he'll come and tell you as well." As I made my way home, other Eskimos in the camp told me repeatedly of the dance that was to be held that night. Evidently there was great anticipation throughout the camp.

It was a beautifully calm, still evening, and I was looking out the window at a glorious sunset, when around the corner of the house came Putnai. There was no mistake whose son he was; he looked a miniature Ootoroot. "We're going to dance," he said. "Hurry up and come. I'm going to tell the rest." And away he sped to the tents by the seashore.

There was no need to hurry, for no one was going yet, but soon men and women by ones and twos slowly made their way to Ootoroot's tent. The light was almost gone and hardly a sound was to be heard from the camps except the chatter of children as they played. Now and then a single dog howled, to be joined almost instantly by every dog in the village.

Boom! Boom! Boom! The sound of the drum reverberated through the very cold and still night air. I noticed the sea ice still fast to the shore. Slipping on my parka, I made my way to the camp. Having successfully negotiated many rows of dogs tethered close by, I pulled back the tent flap. For a moment the lamp light blinded me and I could make out little. Someone said, "Come in," and a hand drew me forward and sideways, and I stumbled in over the legs of people squatting on the floor. Ootoroot beckoned to me, and in a second or two I was seated on the caribou skins at his side.

Kootneak, an old man, was drumming, and I whispered to my host asking if he had yet drummed. "No," he replied. "The oldest man drums first, then the next oldest and so on, with the young lads drumming last."

It was a strange sight. In the very centre crouched old Kootneak, the drum held upright in his left hand and the drumstick swinging in his right hand. With it he hit the rim of the drum with the right side of the handle, causing the drum to revolve on its own axis, then he hit the left side as it swung toward him. At each blow he bobbed up and down and moved around in a small circle with little hopping steps. His long hair streamed in the current of air made by his energetic movements and the rotation of the drum, while the tail of his attigi swayed back and forth with each movement of his body. The huge shadow thrown by the drum and his figure danced across the surface of the bell-like tent, now almost blotting out the faces of men and women, and a second later throwing them into relief and others into shade.

In perfect unison the women swayed slightly forward and backward as they chanted Kootneak's song. The half light, their streaming hair and colourful hairsticks seemed to make the chant of their song even more exotic. They sang one stanza in a monotone, adding "aya ya, aya ya ya, aya ya," then the next stanza and again the interminable "aya ya." Some of the women had a child asleep in the pouch on their backs, but the majority had left their small children at home.

Outside this circle of women, the men sat or lounged, watching the drummer, most of them smoking, so that in a short while the tent was hazy with tobacco smoke, which only added to the character of the scene.

I shut my eyes and listened. Gradually the drum beats slowed down as the chant dropped to a lower key and then ceased altogether. After a few light taps on the skin of the drum, Kootneak carefully laid both the drum and stick (kutook) on the floor, and stepping over the ring of singers, he resumed his place at the back of the tent.

After a short pause, several of the men called to Ootoroot to drum. In accordance with good taste he said, "No, I do not know how to drum," at which they pressed him all the more. At last he rose and stepped into the centre, picking up the drum with slow, deliberate movements. Holding it as Kootneak had, he lightly touched its surface with the stick and said the first word of his song. Then he stopped and said, "I am no good." Peering into the apex of the tent as if seeking inspiration, he lightly tapped the drum again, this time managing to start the first two words of his song. Suddenly he stopped and said, "My memory is bad; I cannot remember."

169

Ootoroot bobs and sways as he performs his drum dance. The squatting women encircle him, chanting and swaying to the rhythmic beat.

A slight pause ensued and at last he started to sing his song. At the second stanza his wife began to sing and as if this was a signal, all the women joined in. Ootoroot now stopped singing. The tempo rose and he beat the drum more strongly than ever until it seemed that the drum could hardly withstand the force of the blows. Every now and then he would yell "Oi" at the top of his voice and beat harder. By this time he was swaying to and fro with each beat, entirely oblivious to anything but his dance. On and on went the drumming until at last the song ended and Ootoroot tapped the drum lightly to signal his finish. But his wife had decided otherwise, for she started another song in which the rest of the women joined, and Ootoroot had to continue.

Three times this happened; as time went on Ootoroot would pause at intervals and tap the surface of the drum, only to resume his beating even more violently than before. At last he laid down the drum and returned to his place, perspiration running down his face, for the atmosphere of the tent was almost overpowering with so many crowded into such a small space, and his violent exertion had made him hotter than ever. Another man soon took his place, and the dance went on. One after another the men drummed, for as soon as one finished another took his place.

I timed several of them to see how long they kept up such sustained exertion. Several of them beat for four minutes at a stretch, which is no small feat, because the drum has to be held freely in the hand with no other support.

At midnight I left and went home to bed, and even as I fell asleep I could still hear the distant, rhythmic throbbing of the drum, which would continue until dawn lightened the eastern sky. Only then would the people wearily make their way home to their tents to sleep out the remainder of the long day.

Perhaps at sundown they would have another dance.

COAT FASHIONS AND OTHER ART

This time of gathering together for the brief spring and summer seasons is also a good time to observe and admire the Padlimuits' extraordinary coats — stylish, fashionable, and with tails! The great variety of fashions represented a wide territory in any settlement. It's a simple matter, when you meet a stranger, to recognize his or her tribe. The peak on top of the hood, for example, is a symbol of a certain tribe, but it also has a definite function. The outer coat (kooli-tak) has a draw string around the front of the hood, and when drawn tight, it's kept in place by simply hooking the excess string (always tied in a loop) over the top of the peak. Tied in that way, the hood stays snug about the face.

One thing that strikes a visitor to the North as much as anything else is the lack of colour in the dress and in the lives of the Eskimos (except for the goods bought in trading stores, such as red woollen blankets, brightly coloured prints, silk handkerchiefs, beads, etc.). But even so, Eskimos created beautiful and subtle combinations of browns and white. Inner coats have the fur turned next to the body, whereas the outer coat has the fur to the outside, and some are paneled. The sole decoration of coats before the traders came lay in the various colours of caribou skins. Dark, chocolate-brown skins have always been greatly favoured for outside coats, for the white fur from the belly contrasts well with such skins and is skilfully used to make effective patterning. Such coats are trimmed around the lower edge and often

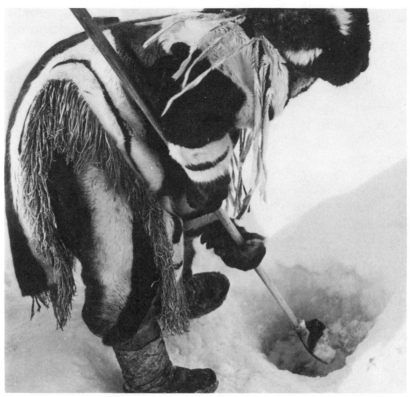

A young woman scoops fresh water from an ice hole. Her clothes are a beautiful creation of dark brown and white caribou skins in typical yet distinctive designs and patterns.

have a white strip around the hood. For appearance and to aid the cut, three square or oblong panels are let into men's coats across the shoulders.

Many Eskimo men have two or more coats, and usually one of them has no paneling at all. The more paneling in a garment, the colder it is, since after a time the skins dry out and the stitches stretch; soon cold draughts start to filter through, particularly in the area of the shoulders.

When the weather begins to get warm (around zero degrees Fahrenheit or a little above), out come the new coats made from the lightweight summer skins. The spring parade of new coats and finery isn't confined to the fashion-conscious South. Husbands whose wives desire to honour them appear resplendent in these coats, and they self-consciously visit from camp to camp.

All coats of summer skin or the heavier fall hides have fringes around the bottom of their tails. This fringe is made from the skin of the caribou's white belly. After the hair is removed, the hide is cut or fringed to a depth of about three inches, leaving a narrow half-inch band which holds the fringe together and which is sewn into the garment. Fringes are found on every coat for all ages and both sexes, and these fringes ensure that only a gentle breath of air can find its way inside to the wearer's body. Without this ventilation the wearer would be either too hot or too cold. The only reason for a fringe to be missing is because of a taboo that dictates that if the wearer is an inlander, the fringing must be ripped off when he reaches the coast, because it's here that land and sea meet; bad hunting will result if the taboo isn't observed. (This taboo doesn't apply to every tribe.)

Among the far northern Eskimos, white caribou skin is inserted in each side of the coat's front. These two panels represent walrus tusks. Caribou Eskimos, however, don't follow this practice, though the same design is always used as a main outline for decoration of their beaded coats.

Some of the main differences in cut can be seen in the coats of the Caribou Eskimos as compared with those of the more northerly Aivilingmiut, at Repulse Bay. The Padlimiut cut their tails so that one falls in front and the other (slightly longer) in back. The northerners have the split between the two tails at the front and back so that the flaps will cover the hips.

The tails of the young men from southern tribes are quite different. They are cut high above the hips and look very distinctive, especially when a youth turns around, lifts his train and ties it up to a string hanging from his waist so that it's completely out of the way. Such a tail is very useful to sit on when traveling on a sled. If a coat tail is cut too short, it will wrinkle or ruck up when sat upon and allow the cold wind to chase around inside.

One most important difference between a coat made by an Eskimo and one tailored on Fifth Avenue in New York is that the latter tailor does his utmost to ensure that the coat fits snugly across the shoulders without wrinkle or blemish. An Eskimo wife, however, doesn't concern herself with such minor details. To her — and her husband as well — the all-important thing is whether or not one's arms can be pulled out of the sleeves without pulling the coat over the head.

This may sound a little strange, but I can assure you that to sit in an unheated igloo from noon till night with the temperature well below zero isn't pleasant, and though you would hardly consider yourself comfortable or even warm when you pull your arms from the sleeves and place them against your body, at least your hands become less blue and gain some semblance of warmth.

The foregoing concerns men's wear, but it can be applied as well to women's coats, which are much more interesting for several reasons. First, there's that long baggy hood that hangs down to or even below the waist. The hood has some use as a bag for such articles as a woman's ulu, tobacco, matches and pipe, but its main use is for protection of the baby. The baby, of course, is in the pouch (amaot) and not in the hood itself. Pictures seldom show the pouch, as the hood hides it. Indoors (or even outdoors on fine days) the baby is quite comfortable with its head free so that it can look around. When the wind blows or it's cold, the mother draws the hood forward over her own head and folds it toward the windward side. With these three thicknesses of fur, the baby has perfect protection. Around mother's face the hood is open a little, making a small opening through which the child can breathe and see. Lying naked on mother's bare back, small babies have their legs crossed beneath them in the pouch. Older children are sometimes carried, but usually only when they're sick; in that case their legs hang down and the support thong passes beneath the knees and under the amaot.

The shape of the tails of a woman's coat denotes the wearer's tribe and whether or not she's married or has been a mother. Designs range from long, almost pointed flaps of beautiful lines to square-cut, stubby tails, all of which touch or almost touch the ground. The front tail is much smaller than the back, of course, and even these vary in size and shape with the different tribes. Both front and rear tails are solely for utilitarian purposes. A nursing infant sits on mother's lap enfolded in the inturned front flap or tail, which makes a warm, furry bed where no draught can creep up the edge of the coat. The back flap provides a large expanse of fur below the pouch when the baby is carried, and so to a great extent this ensures a draught-free seat, especially when mother sits down. When traveling, the woman sits on the back tail or flap.

174

The coat worn by women or girls who've never borne a child is without a pouch and has a square-cut end to the back tail. This end has no fringes; it is rolled inwards and held in this position by two strings of skin (or in modern days, of plaited wool) which are attached from the corners to just below the shoulders of the coat, under the hood.

Outer coats are often wonderfully paneled. Sometimes strings of white caribou skin hang from the shoulders of the coat, enhancing the wildness of the attire and giving it additional beauty. Although there are tribal ways of paneling, not all coats are alike within a tribe. The paneling may be narrow or wide and range in colour from pure white through shades of a delicate golden brown to dark brown. The southern Eskimos panel their sleeves with vertical strips of any width that appeals to the seamstress, while the northerners panel theirs with horizontal strips. In the infinite variety and beauty that are all their own, the coats of the women indicate the personal taste and patience of their owners. Garments aren't inspected to see if they're prettier than a neighbour's, but rather to see if the skins are as soft and the stitches as small.

I recall one day when school was in progress. There on long benches perched little Eskimo children either studiously sucking their pencils as they tried to remember their Eskimo alphabet or, with pencils in clenched fists, attempting to print these characters in their exercise books. Boys were on one side of the room and girls on the other, as is the custom among the Eskimos. From their little rears hung a line of tails. I looked and then looked again. Not one of them had the same size and shape of tail. The smaller the child, the smaller the tail, and the larger he or she was, the larger the tail had grown. One of the boys of about ten years old even had a long-tailed coat.

Coats play a great part in the lives of the Eskimos, from childhood to old age. Tiny babies, of course, own nothing. They have to be old enough to sit upright before they graduate to the stage of wearing a deerskin or cloth hat or bonnet, their first real clothing. Even when only six months old, a child may be put down on a sleeping bag in temperatures around zero wearing nothing more than the cosy bonnet and, amazingly, the child seems quite warm. Such bonnets are usually paneled and are of different styles, depending on the infant's sex. When the child gets to the stage where he wants to see everything going on around him, mother will put a

An older sister takes her young charge along with her to school. The child's coat is short and the overall-type pants are big and baggy, with a cut-away "convenience" feature. The back tail of the young girl's outer coat is square-cut, indicating that she is not married; her coat has a hood but no pouch.

fringe on his hat to keep a certain amount of draught from the hood opening.

This stage really is the start of a coat, for after all, the hat is actually a hood, and the body and arms of the coat are added when the child gets older and graduates to a little coat with a straight edge all around the bottom. The youngster wears this coat until it becomes a pair of pants and socks (all in one piece). Then the little tail at the back starts to grow and keeps pace with the child, and after a time the front tail emerges (with the girls). At the age of puberty, the boys wear coats like their fathers' and the girls wear the long-tailed (upturned) variety without the pouch. This coat gives way to a woman's with the birth of the first child, for then a coat with a pouch is necessary.

A coveted and greatly prized item used in clothing decoration is the coloured seed bead, introduced by white traders into the North. The Eskimo women are exceptionally clever in their choice and combination of the bright, primary-coloured beads. Their expert craftsmanship blends these in perfect harmony to produce geometrical designs of amazing beauty.

One day in 1938 Attarchuk arrived at our house with her husband and relatives. She stood resplendent in a new, beautifully beaded coat. We asked, "Where's the coat you wore last year?" Shrugging her shoulders, she feigned not understanding, then with a laugh she said, "Oh, I undid all the beadwork and made this instead." "Why?" we asked. "Because I needed the beads."

Among her collection of beads were very old, larger ones that must have been bartered at the turn of the century. We offered to buy her as many beads — and more — that she might need for another coat if she would sell us her beautiful coat. She agreed, and now that coat resides for all to view in the Museum of Man and Nature in Winnipeg.

Surprisingly, the marvelously artistic ornamentation that made Padlimiut coats so distinctive seemed absent in almost all other areas of their lives. Eskimos who lived farther north, on the edge of the Arctic Ocean and in even more severe living conditions, treasured small pieces of wood and their relatively few animal products; but they often created pieces of art from these wooden bits, from ivory tusks, and from soapstone. The Padlimiut, in a land of relative plenty, almost

Attarchuk in her wonderfully beaded attigi. This coat is now permanently housed in the Museum of Man and Nature in Winnipeg.

never carved anything that could be called "art," though antlers and skins were plentiful and wood could be rather easily obtained. Pottery has been found among some remains of old Eskimo houses, although none has ever been found among the Padlimiut.

The Padlimiut seemed generally not to take pride in how they made tools, weapons, or utensils and they made them without decoration. Of all the articles I've ever seen made by these people or their forefathers, only one had even circles carved on it, and these were likely made with a modern bit, as the hole in the centre could be plainly seen. The article was made from walrus tusk, perhaps left behind by a visitor from a northern tribe.

Yet, there remains one avenue for artistic expression, and that's in the figures that they cut out from skin, paper, or cloth to stick on their igloo walls. The cut-outs resemble the drawings of so-called "primitive man" found elsewhere in caves and cliff dwellings. Unfortunately, there's no evidence as to whether this is a modern practice introduced by the white men or one that has survived for centuries, since the summer dwellings of these people have been mostly tents and their snow dwellings melted readily in the spring sunshine.

A form of Padlimiut sculpture is found in the bird decoys used for attracting ducks and geese. These are very realistic, but here again it's questionable whether or not these date from early times. Such decoys are usually made from bundles of moss, with sticks for necks and heads; they recall the paramount importance of food in the economy of Arctic living.

If and when life in the Arctic should become less rigorous, less of a struggle to maintain life itself, perhaps then we may expect to find an increase in the art of the Padlimiut Eskimos. The exquisite Padlimiut coats, however, more than compensate for the lack of art work in other areas of their lives.

Fall moving day at Eskimo Point. Interested onlookers watch several families organize their boats for a journey of some fifty miles northward along the coast to Maguse River to meet the caribou migration inland. Others will walk inland, carrying all their belongings, to their winter sites. Note the dogs in one of the canoes; liable to seasickness, the usually antisocial dogs seldom fought in the canoes.

CHAPTER NINE
LATE FALL: MOVING DAY

Too soon for anyone's liking summer was gone. Nights became dreadfully cold and snow began to fall at Eskimo Point. The tents had to be taken down and the individual family migrations to the inland igloo sites organized.

Late one fall I arrived at Punagooneak's camp, some distance from the mission, just as he had decided to abandon tent life and build his winter snow house. Punagooneak had chosen a place that promised to be a good location. Let the winter come; he would build an igloo for himself, for his family, and for the others. It would be a communal igloo, possibly for three families, with one entrance. To have an igloo at last, after living in a tent all summer! It had been very cold lately; the thermometer had hovered probably at fifteen degrees below zero for several days.

For two days Punagooneak had been busy building his igloo. First he'd probed the snow with a three-foot-long stick tipped with walrus ivory, until he found a place where the snow was of the same texture to a depth of two feet. He had cut two deep, parallel channels with his snow knife about three feet apart and then, cutting out a wedge at one end, he was able to get his snow knife down far enough to cut the bottom of his blocks about twenty inches deep. Marking the depth of the block with a line, he forced the blade of his snow knife downwards along this mark with quick stabs. With a motion thrusting downward and outward, he split free the block of snow, a perfect tablet. Block after block followed in quick succession until he had a channel cut across the entire diameter of his proposed igloo, about twenty-seven feet. He made another series of blocks at right angles to the first trench, forming a cross. Now a mass of snow blocks lay around; these he arranged in a circle.

When this was completed he trimmed the first few blocks so that they sloped upwards from the ground. His second tier rose along this line, followed by a third tier, in turn followed by a fourth. Soon after he started on his third row, he had to cut his way out, finishing with blocks cut from outside. These were thicker, by about six inches or so, to give better protection. Punagooneak was now ready to move. He had made the walls upright in Padlimiut style, unlike the dome-shaped structures common to most Eskimo tribes which are the popular notion of an Eskimo igloo.

When he announced to his wife that the igloo was ready for the move, she rushed across to the other tents calling her friends to come and help her. As usual, the children of the camp arrived to share the excitement with Punagooneak's little ones. The wind was strong and it was snowing. Because of the wind, all the women had their hoods draped over the windward side of their heads as they hurried over to help.

First they unlaced the front opening of the tent a little, and while Heeamrook was busy at this job, Koomuk tried to

Satisfied that the igloo is ready, Punagooneak comes to tell his wife it's time to move. The igloo is visible in the background, its straight-sided walls ready to receive the tent poles as rafters. Summer's tent stands at right, while a snowdrift rises at left.

remove the anchor stones that lay around the outside bottom of the tent. They were frozen solidly and had to be hit with an axe before they parted from their beds. Starting at the tent flap, Keeamook and Koomuk attempted to release the tent covering from the ground. It too was frozen fast. After a little tugging, part of it gave way so suddenly that they almost fell backwards. This was great fun and caused considerable laughter. Pulling was out of the question, for the more they pulled the more the bottom tore. Once again armed with axes, they chopped away the frozen earth and eventually freed the tent. As Punagooneak pulled on the back of the tent to free it, the increasing wind filled it and the whole suddenly gave and billowed out into the wind. Everyone rushed to help and hold it down while Heeamrook climbed onto a box to release the rest of the lacing at the front. With all hands hauling on it, they soon had the tent covering spread out on a snow bank, where the children beat it to remove the snow. The tent poles now stood out starkly against the grey sky.

Neelookark, a young lad, ran up and untied the pieces of skin line that hung down one pole and held the tent structure together; he ran around and around the poles, unwinding the line. Each circuit freed a tent pole, which one of the men grasped immediately and carried to the igloo. Neelookark continued his round, often stumbling over lumps of snow or stones, greatly to the amusement of the others. Unlike southerners, an Eskimo doesn't mind being laughed at; he too joins in the fun.

While the men were taking the poles over to the igloo, the women brought the bed skins, bags of clothing, and various other larger articles, all of which they pitched over the wall onto the sleeping bench of snow.

The two men of the camp, Pungakayoo and Punagooneak, next laid all the poles parallel to each other, like rafters, across the top of the igloo at about ten inches apart. Then with their snow knives they cut little grooves into the snow wall and let the poles fall into them, making the top of the poles level with the top of the snow wall. Everyone now took hold of one side of the tent cover, and by flapping it — and aided by the wind — they shook off all the loose snow. Then the men folded it twice, turning the ends over onto the middle. This unwieldy bundle they dragged to the side of the igloo, lifted above their heads, and slid onto the poles. Standing on blocks of snow, they unfolded the tent

183

cover and carefully adjusted it to cover the top of the igloo. Any portions that hung over the sides they folded onto the top. Pungakayoo then lifted previously cut snow blocks and arranged them around the outer edge of the tent cover so that their weight was supported by the walls. In this position they soon froze and so held down the covering.

In the meantime the women had been busy inside, beating the bed skins and spare suits of clothing with a snow beater, afterwards laying them on the "mattress." The Eskimo mattress is a bundle of branches from the willow shrub, about two feet long and sewn together with sinew, then made into a large mat — or several mats — large enough to cover the whole of the sleeping bench in a tent or igloo. This article prevents bed skins from having direct contact with the snow.

With the sleeping bench tidy, the women took the rest of the belongings in through the door, which at this point was merely a hole cut in the wall.

What an indescribable mess was left at the tent site! Old bones, bits of skin, fragments of meat, little bits of wood, wooden dishes, old clothes, and a thousand and one odd things. Rifles, dog harnesses, whip, and such things were thrown onto the top of the igloo by Punagooneak, so as to be out of the dogs' reach. Leaving the women to their work of cleaning up and putting things in order at home, he set to work and in half an hour had built a protecting porch with a dome of snow. Moving day was over.

The next day a fierce gale blew. It was impossible to see a yard through the blinding, stinging, whirling snow. The particles of snow, driving with unrelenting force, cut through some of the blocks at the top of the igloo; at first a hole only a pin-point in size appeared. Snow drove in to settle in a layer of white over the sleeping bench. Soon a small mound formed as the hole became larger, and others appeared. Punagooneak had to go outside to stuff snow into the holes. Heeamrook used mitts, odd bits of deerskin — anything to stop them up on the inside.

By morning the storm began to abate, and before noon the wind had dropped almost entirely. As it happened, the top row of blocks had been worn very thin, so that there was nothing to be done but to take off the roof again and put on a fresh layer of blocks. All went well, and before nightfall the igloo was snug once more. Winter had arrived again.

After the storm. The new igloos are already well covered with snow blown onto them. Winter is here again.

EPILOGUE

Yearly the seasons came and went, even as now, once more, winter was encompassing the camp of Punagooneak. Unforeseen and lurking in the darkening shadows and terrible blizzards there stalked the spectre of change. For only a few more years would the traditional life of the Eskimos continue. Hitherto we had been able to cope with illness and epidemics, but in the mid-1940s and on, the white people's diseases and widespread starvation simply decimated the Inuit. Starvation had been known to them since time immemorial, but it usually affected only a few in specific areas. But the continuing spread of starvation and the consequent erosion of health, including widespread dog disease, hit all Eskimos, including the Padlimiut. These had such a devastating effect that survival depended on government action to airlift whole communities into settlements. Seven hundred Eskimos of Cumberland Gulf were moved to Pangnirtung; in the early 1950s Eskimo Point became a permanent settlement for the stricken Padlimiut. Temporary government relief measures provided both food rations and a length of canvas for a meagre tent. The old way seemed at an end. The once proud, independent Inuk was left bereft and stripped of his noble way of life. His dogs were gone, his family life in shambles. Death had claimed many.

In the spring of 1944 we had moved on to Aklavik in the western Arctic. There, as archdeacon, Donald ministered to Eskimos, Loucheux Indians, and Whites. He succeeded Bishop Archibald Fleming in 1950, becoming second bishop of the Arctic. It was during subsequent lengthy visitations within the diocese that he witnessed first-hand the magnitude of the devastation which had hit all the Eskimo people, and he marveled at their indomitable will to survive. He was destined to serve them for another two decades. They were the love of his life — these, the bravest people on earth — the Inuit.